Lebanon

The
Business Traveller's
Handbook

Lebanon
The Business Traveller's Handbook

First published in 2003 by
Interlink Books
An imprint of Interlink Publishing Group, Inc.
46 Crosby Street, Northampton, Massachusetts 01060
www.interlinkbooks.com

ISBN 1-56656-496-4

Library of Congress Cataloging-in-Publication Data available

The author and publisher have made every effort to ensure that the facts in this handbook are accurate and up-to-date. The reader is advised, however, to verify travel and visa arrangements with the appropriate consular office prior to departure. The author and publisher cannot accept any responsibility for loss, injury or inconvenience, however caused.

None of the maps in this book are designed to have any political significance.

Printed and bound in Singapore by Tien Wah Press

To request our complete 40-page full-color catalog, please call us toll free at 1-800-238-LINK, visit our website at www.interlinkbooks.com or send us an e-mail: info@interlinkbooks.com

PICTURE CREDITS: *Title page*, Bernard Saikalis; *page 4 (t) page 5 (b)* Barbara Thomason; *page 7*, Solidere

Lebanon

The Business Travellers' Handbook

George Asseily
&
James Lawday

The waterfall in the pretty valley of 'Basatin al-'Issi', 85 kilometres north of Beirut, sends water plunging some 50 metres into the verdant valley below, ever popular with hikers and campers.

The Temple of Bacchus in Baalbek is probably the best preserved Roman Temple in the Middle East.

The Palace of Beiteddine, one of the famous decorative doors constructed in 1812 during the reign of Emir Bechir Chehab II.

Above: 'Le Grand Sérail,' offices of the Prime Minister in downtown Beirut. It is a grandiose example of the Ottoman presence.

Opposite: The development of Beirut Central District is one of the most ambitious postwar reconstruction and urban regeneration ventures of our time.

Below: The streets of downtown Beirut were rebuilt following the war, and now serve as an attractive hub for the city's business and social life.

SOLIDERE. Developing the *finest* city center in the Middle East.

A concept and vision turned into reality

Beirut city center

Pedestrianized historic core, green spaces
Banks, offices, embassies, regional agencies
Beirut Souks,shopping, restaurants, entertainment
Urban villages, friendly environment
Beirut Marina, waterfront residential, hotels
Wonderful investment opportunities

SOLIDERE

Foreword

the Rt. Hon. Lord Eden of Winton PC
Formerly Minister for Industry, Minister of Posts and
Telecommunications and Chairman of the
British Lebanese Association

Lebanon is a land of great beauty and contrast; its origins are buried deep in history; and the many influences of landscape, culture and conflict have helped to form the character of its people. It is a fascinating country to visit and an exciting place in which to do business.

After the tragic years of self-destruction and foreign incursion, Lebanon is once again emerging as the financial, commercial and recreational centre of the Middle East. The work of reconstruction is well advanced, communications have been modernised and Beirut itself is being sensitively restored. The fast direct motorway from the new airport ensures a frustration-free transfer to the city centre.

The opportunities for business are considerable. Tourism is a major growth area, agriculture – especially the long-established and widely acclaimed wine industry – is another. Every activity and product associated with building, construction and communication offer enormous scope for new business. Education, media and health are other prime areas. The financial sector is strong, banking being a major contribution to the national GDP, while the attitude of government departments to the incoming businessmen is positive and encouraging. The Lebanese generally are eager and willing to help, they are a wonderfully-diversified, colourful and warm-hearted people with a great sense of national pride and a passionate drive to help in the rehabilitation of their country.

Two distinguished and experienced businessmen, James Lawday and George Asseily, have come together to prepare this handbook for the Business Traveller to Lebanon – a worthy addition to the excellent series from the Gorilla Guides. The result is an immensely practical guide packed with useful information and sound advice. Anyone planning to do business in Lebanon will find it a real asset and a reliable companion.

CONTENTS

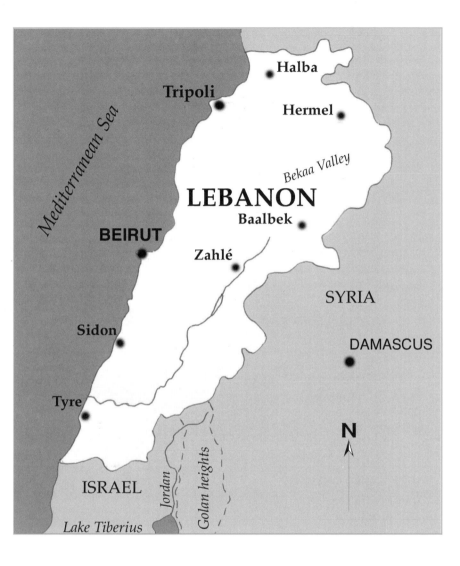

Lebanon

1

Lebanon yesterday and today

Lebanon yesterday and today

1

Lebanon and the Lebanese

A land of milk and honey? A land of war and peace? A land of hard work and leisure? Yes indeed, Lebanon is all these and of course much more. Lebanon, sometimes described as the Riviera of the Middle East, is one of the jewels of the region and a Mediterranean playground, albeit now scarred by the conflicts of recent decades.

Situated at the extreme east of the Mediterranean, and sandwiched between Syria and Israel, Lebanon is a very small country – smaller than Wales. The east of the country is bordered by Syria and the range of mountains known as Anti Lebanon and the Bekaa Valley, a valley with its own mystery of wine and drugs, of warlords and freedom fighters, of remains of ancient civilisations and famous music festivals. The capital of Lebanon, Beirut, is situated on a promontory of land protruding into the Mediterranean about midway along its coastline. The highest mountains of Lebanon remain snow covered for most of the year and make a dramatic backdrop for the city of Beirut.

1

The Lebanese International Community

Go to any corner of the world and there will always be a close-knit Lebanese community. These communities will inevitably include successful entrepreneurs and businessmen who in their brief time in their adopted country almost invariably left some mark. It is suggested that there are more Lebanese living overseas than actually live in their own country. However the majority of these will not forget their roots and hope one day to return to their homeland.

Entrepreneurs

Why is Lebanon special, as indeed it is? Perhaps the combination of its people resourceful, hard working, hedonistic, perspicacious and aggressive, and the country's geography; dramatic and yet gently interesting, make Lebanon what it is. Maybe its long history of culture, trade and conflict dating back to the beginning of time, have formed the country into the modern Lebanon of the second millennium.

1

Lebanon has had a disproportionate influence on regional and world affairs. It is situated at the start of the Silk Route, which led to the fabulous riches of the Far East. Today as the most eastern country on the Mediterranean it still offers an overland route from Europe and America to the Middle East.

The famous Cedars of Lebanon, immortalised on its national flag, have for thousands of years been the source of timber in the ancient world. In a region where few major sources of timber existed, Lebanon became an important exporter of this essential commodity and evidence of this durable timber remains to this day as far afield as the temples and palaces of the Pharaohs. Sadly, now only a handful of these magnificent trees are still standing.

Lebanon has had few other natural resources to support its population: neither oil nor gas, nor any of the other natural minerals which have provided the wealth of so many of its Arab neighbours. Indeed Lebanon is not a wealthy country. Its real resource has, however, been its people and their way of life. It is this entrepreneural spirit that – coupled – with its outstanding East-West strategic location – made Beirut the logical location for international companies to establish a regional office in the 1950s and 1960s. Transport and communications were good and so was the quality of life. But the turbulence in the country in the 1970s and 1980s combined with the globalisation of modern communications have led to the departure of most major international corporations.

Lebanon is very European in its outlook. For example, the business week is Monday to Friday, unlike the rest of the Middle East, and working hours tend to be similar to Europe. Most Lebanese, in addition to their very smart and classical Arabic, speak English and French. Western dress is the norm for both business and leisure.

Lebanon therefore relies on its human natural resources. Lebanon is about the Lebanese who are the main industry and export. Whether as bankers, as businessmen, as traders, importers and exporters, the Lebanese community around the world will ensure its survival. Services are what Lebanon offers to the world and any visitor can soon experience such services within minutes of arriving at Beirut Airport. Industry in Lebanon consists of small and medium sized institutions involved mostly in textiles, leather, ceramics, building materials, pharmaceuticals and jewellery – as well as food industries. The most noteworthy exports are the excellent wines that are made locally. The industry with the greatest potential for growth is tourism.

A Brief History of Lebanon

The first significant settlers established settlements along the coast of Lebanon, with Byblos and Tyre being the most important, and Beirut and Sidon. These city-states became the hubs of the Canaanite civilisation. The Egyptian Pharaohs swept through and invaded around 1500 BC and with their gradual demise the Canaanites reformed as a merchant trading civilisation. By 1,000 BC their influence had spread widely and they came to be known as the Phoenicians.

For about four centuries the **Phoenicians** developed their trading, exploration and colonisation throughout the Mediterranean Sea, spreading their culture and goods. Their skills of navigation and seamanship became legendary and their influence spread, from Carthage and Utica in North Africa to Cadiz in Spain. There are even suggestions that they may have reached as far west as Cornwall in the UK and as far east as India, possibly circumnavigating the African continent. Perhaps as a result of this trading and travelling they developed an alphabet to replace the complicated cuneiform and hieroglyphic scripts they had inherited. This new simplified form of recording events became the basis for the Greek script and subsequently, via Latin, for all European written languages.

The Phoenicians were also significant manufacturers. Metalwork, textile and glass products became major exports for the country as well as for home consumption, with products from Sidon being particularly famous. However it was the Phoenicians' discovery of a purple dye, which they extracted from a seashell, that really made their fortunes. We will all recall the pictures of the purple robes, which were worn by royalty and senior figures in Rome and Athens.

Sadly, there are few traces of this civilisation left today. A few artefacts and remains (of temple and jetty) have been found at Byblos and Tyre and there have been some

The Phoenicians

1

significant finds – Phoenician walls – during the reconstruction of the new city centre of Beirut. However, the bulk of our knowledge of the Phoenicians comes from writers at that time, Homer and Herodotus, with further insights from the Bible.

The advent of the **Assyrians** in the 8th century BC, taking control of some of the city states, including Byblos and Tyre, saw the Phoenician regional dominance of trade come to an end. For about three hundred years this decline continued with the Assyrians being replaced by Babylonians. A revival of their fortunes occurred when the **Persians** arrived around 6th century BC, with Phoenicia becoming the most prosperous region in the Persian Empire. This lasted for another two hundred years until **Alexander the Great** swept through the region in 333 BC.

Greeks

Alexander's army conquered the city-states of Phoenicia. All of them, except Tyre submitted immediately to the **Greeks**. After a siege lasting several months Tyre also submitted, but not without massive damage to the city and loss of life of its population. The Greeks rebuilt the city as a Macedonian fortress. The culture of Phoenicia now declined, being replaced by Greek laws, customs and its religion. On the death of Alexander in 323 BC, the Greek's conquests were divided up amongst three generals, with Palestine, Egypt and Phoenicia coming under the rule of Ptolemy I. Much fighting amongst the generals and their followers ensued for the next hundred years until in 200 BC the Seleucids ousted the followers of Ptolemy from Phoenicia. Greek civilisation remained dominant in the region for many years, but was no match for the military might of the Roman Empire.

Romans

In 64 BC the Roman armies conquered Phoenicia following a three-year campaign. The country, together with Palestine, became part of the regional province of Syria. Beirut became an important capital and the Romans extended and rebuilt the local temple in the religious centre of Baalbek. Roman Gods replaced the Greek and Phoenician pantheon. The Phoenicians developed closer ties with Syria and adopted their language.

Christianity

In AD 329 the Emperor **Constantine** established Christianity as the new religion of the Roman Empire and the capital re-named was moved from Rome to Byzantium, Constantinople.

The form Christianity should take was a subject which occupied much thought during this time. In AD 451 the Council of Chalcedon tried to define the future form of Christianity, which was generally adopted. Controversy continued until in the 7th century a group of Syrian Christians broke away from the generally adopted Church and formed the **Maronites**, the dominant Christian sect in Lebanon today.

The first seven centuries after Christ were fairly quiet in the region. However turmoil arrived in the 7th century, when the followers of the Prophet Mohammed started to conquer the region, driving out the Romans/Byzantines and converting the people to Islam. Shortly afterwards, the Umayyad Caliphate made their capital in Damascus and in the 8th century the Abbasids switched the seat of the Islamic Caliphate to Baghdad. By the end of the 10th century the **Fatimids**, Shiite Muslims, swept across from Egypt to take control of Lebanon, Syria and Palestine. In 1016 the Fatimid Caliph, Al Hakim, declared himself to be the earthly reincarnation of God, which received little support except from a small band of followers in Syria who broke away from the main religious beliefs to follow Al Hakim. This group based themselves in the Mount Lebanon region, south of Beirut, and subsequently became known as the **Druze**, another significant religious force in Lebanon today.

Islam

Gradually the Fatimids in Egypt began to loose control, until at the end of the 11th century tribal leaders from Persia who were supporters of the Caliph in Baghdad restored Sunni Islam. They ruled first from Aleppo and then divided the region into two with centres in Aleppo and Damascus. This fragmented region was ill equipped to defend itself so that by the end of the 11th century the Crusaders swept through the country from the North on their way to liberate Jerusalem. The Maronites gratefully welcomed the Christian armies, even recognising Rome as the head of their church, and saw them as saviours who would return Christian rule to the area. The Muslims – Druze, Shiite and Sunni – threw in their lot with the remnants of the Islamic forces from Aleppo and Damascus.

Crusaders

By the middle of the 12th century the Muslim forces had once again taken control of the region. Ruling from the

1

Saladin | Fatimid court of Egypt, Salah ud-Din (Saladin) went on to regain the land lost to the Crusaders, so that by the end of the 13th century the last of the Crusaders were finally driven away. His slave soldiers, who ruled the region for another three hundred years and became known as the **Mamelukes**, overthrew Salah ud-Din's Ayyubid dynasty in the mid 13th century.

Ottoman conquerors from Constantinople arrived in the Mount Lebanon region in the early 16th century. One of their local governors, **Fakhreddine,** (Fakhr ud-Din) an ambitious and talented man, unified the current area known as Lebanon. He over-extended himself with attempts to rule the surrounding countries so that his Ottoman superiors finally captured and executed him, replacing him with another local leader. The **Shihab** family, who retained the land under an agreement with the Ottomans, then ruled the central areas of the country. A Sunni Muslim family, they cultivated the Druze in the Chouf mountains and looked also for support from the Maronites. By the end of the 18th century the Christian Maronites had persuaded the Shihab family to convert to Christianity, whilst maintaining good relationships with the Ottoman masters in Constantinople and the governors of coastal towns of Lebanon.

Ottomans

The demise of the Shihabs towards the middle of the 19th century was followed by a brief period of instability until the Ottomans decided to divide the area between the Druze and the Maronites. In the 1850s and 1860s hostility between the two groups grew, with fighting and massacres, so that the French, defenders of Christianity, finally intervened, restoring order and introducing a new system of government by the Ottomans. A period of stability followed with the country becoming the academic and cultural centre of the Ottoman world. In 1920 the League of Nations awarded **France** control of Syria and the Mount Lebanon region. Under pressure from the Maronites the French extended control of the area to include all the coastal cities and the Bekaa valley to the East, to form Greater Lebanon. However, growing Arab nationalism in the region and the increase of the Sunni population caused difficulties for the French and their allies until in 1932, the constitution which had been drawn up in 1926 was suspended, with a promise of independence. Following a period of unrest in the 1940s,

1

Lebanon was finally guaranteed **independence** from France in 1943, with an unwritten agreement that the country would be ruled by a Maronite president, a Sunni Prime Minister and the speaker of the parliament a Shiite Muslim. This system of government continues to this day.

Independence

The division of Palestine in 1948 was to be the start of a long-lasting dispute with its southern neighbour. The first Palestinian refugees crossed the border soon after the division as enthusiastic Israelis occupied more land. In the 1950s ties with Syria were finally broken, increasing the financial difficulties in Lebanon. Arab nationalism in the region, with Nasser in Egypt forming a United Arab Republic with Syria on one hand, together with a pro-western Maronite president Chamoun, increased the plight of the Lebanese people. In 1958 Chamoun requested military help from the United States of America who sent 15,000 marines to quell the disturbances between Maronites and Sunnis. Two subsequent presidents tried to reform the country and in some way succeeded, although their efforts and reforms concentrated on the wealthy coastal inhabitants, ignoring the plight of the people in the mountains. This was the 1960s when Lebanon became famous as an international playground.

Division of Palestine

1

Memorials

A unique site in Lebanon is located on the road from Beirut to Tripoli at Jounieh. At some point the road goes through a tunnel under a bluff of rock, which extends to the sea. On the North side of this tunnel is a small river called the Dog River or Nahr al Kalb. This steep rock face has always presented a natural barrier to forces making their way south to Beirut. Whilst waiting to cross armies have left memorials to their adventures carved in stone – military graffiti?

These memorials are located in the cliff face and date back to Ramses II of Egypt. They are in various scripts including Greek, Latin, Arabic, French and English apart from earlier inscriptions. Modern records of British and French armies can be seen and also the more recent forces in the civil war.

Recent History

The most recent events in Lebanon probably started in 1967 with the **6-Day War**, when Israel extended its borders into Egypt (Sinai), Syria (Golan Heights) and Jordan and displaced many more Palestinians, many of whom ended up in Lebanon. In the ensuing years Israel made further incursions into Lebanon and a Palestinian guerrilla movement was born.

Civil War

It was not until 1975 that the **Civil War** started when a Christian faction, the Phalangists, supported at that time by Israel, attacked a bus in South Beirut and murdered 27 Palestinians. Syrian, Iranian, French, Israeli and American forces all took part in fighting in Lebanon in the next 15 years and some spent a lot of time in the country trying to separate the warring factions. Militia groups were formed including Phalangists, Hisbollah, South Lebanese Army, Amal, and the Palestine Liberation Organisation (PLO). Religious groups including Maronite, Druze, Sunni and Shiite were also involved. Beirut was divided into Christian East and Muslim West by the notorious Green Line – so called after the trees and vegetation that soon took hold of this part of the ruined city. One hundred and fifty thousand were killed in the war with nearly 20,000 killed when Israel bombarded Beirut in 1982, and 2,000 massacred in the **Sabra and Chatilla**

Sabra and Chatilla camps by the Phalange in the same year. Incidents like the American shelling of the Druze in the mountains of Beirut and the subsequent bombing of the US Embassy and Marine headquarters in 1983, all made it into the international news, along with the kidnappings of Westerners by the militia. Many Lebanese fled their country and established successful business communities around the world.

Peace Restored

In 1989 the **Taif Accord** brought to an end the strife in Lebanon. Gradually normality returned until in 1992 when all western hostages had been released, elections were held in the country, the first for two decades, and Rafiq Hariri, a Lebanese/Saudi businessman, was elected Prime Minister. Since that time relative peace returned to the country and a massive rebuilding programme was started – a rebuilding programme that not only included bricks and mortar but also institutions and people's lives. Occasional incursions by Israeli forces have occurred since then including attacks on Beirut's infrastructure.

Over 300,000 Palestinian refugees remain in Lebanon and are a constant reminder of the turmoil of the last quarter of the twentieth century.

Lebanon Today

Visitors to Lebanon today will have to look hard if they are to see any signs of the destruction that remained evident in the early 1990s. Beirut itself, which for so long had been synonymous with terror and destruction, is now reasserting itself as a modern Mediterranean city. Old buildings with any architectural merit have been restored; old buildings with no merit at all, especially within the central Beirut district, have been pulled down and new modern developments are rising throughout the country. Inevitably the main thrust of this reconstruction programme is in Beirut, partly because it had seen the most destruction and also because as the capital of the country it stood as an important symbol of regeneration. Tripoli in the North, a sometime haven for fleeing Beirutis, has become a second centre for Lebanon. Jounieh, virtually a suburb of Beirut, and colonised during the more difficult times, is also thriving. In the south of the country the cities of Sidon and Tyre have been slower to become re-established, partly due to their proximity to the southern border with Israel.

Reconstruction

1

Just after the war in the early 1990s vast areas of central Beirut was destroyed, especially those around the Green Line. Hotels, shops, mosques, churches, offices and homes lay in ruins. The airport barely functioned. Water, electricity and telephone services were severely disrupted. Sports facilities were in ruins although the horse race track in Beirut survived intact. The Museum, art galleries and cinemas barely remained. Transport within the country was confused – confused because large areas of Beirut and the country had so long been off limits for citizens (for example, Christian taxi drivers didn't know their way around West Beirut). Although Lebanon sported about 80 different banks, some were no more than privately owned money-boxes and only a few had any substance – a devaluation over the twenty years of the Lebanese pound from 2.5 to the US dollar to a low of 2000 to the dollar, had not increased peoples enthusiasm for banks and their owners.

Renewal

The government of Prime Minister **Rafiq Hariri** embarked upon an ambitious plan for rebuilding the country. International consultants and experts were brought in. Lebanese businessmen, bankers, lawyers, etc,. were persuaded to return to join the government and to join in the planning and implementation of a new restructured Lebanon. Even archaeologists were able to excavate large areas of Beirut, which for so long had remained hidden under centuries of development.

Rapidly Lebanon returned to normal. Hotels opened and business travellers and tourists returned. Business groups from Europe were soon knocking at the doors. While the American government maintained a cautious approach, enterprising but discreet American business executives could be seen in smart hotels. Major international trade exhibitions were held in Beirut and Tripoli. Roads were repaired and new highways built. A new airport was constructed. The port, a significant facility for this trading nation, was opened – such was its efficiency that importers and exporters from the region preferred to use Beirut rather than the other established ports in the region. Government offices reopened – the government reduced taxes across the board and found that they had suddenly an *increase* in revenue! Television and radio stations blossomed and mobile phone networks were installed – Lebanese then became the dubious holders of the record for the most mobile phones per capita in the world.

The wealth and perspicacity of the Lebanese is legendary. Within a short time expensive cars were to be seen on the streets of Lebanon. Luxury hotels opened, offering luxurious surroundings at uncompetitive prices. Restaurants, equivalent in quality to anywhere in the world, were soon overwhelmed by customers. Fast motor cruisers could be seen racing up and down the coastline. Normality and the Lebanese way of life had returned.

Political and financial difficulties returned to the country in the mid 1990s as the burden of the redevelopment programme and political disruption from the southern neighbour reduced financial confidence. A new government in the next decade beleived in a more cautious fiscal policy. However, this slowdown was temporary and a more measured approach to the rebuilding programme continues today.

1

Major Religious Communities in Lebanon

Christians:
    Maronites (Catholic)
    Greek Orthodox
    Greek catholic

Muslim
    Sunni
    Shiite
    Druze

Minorites
    Armenian Catholic
    Armenian Orthodox Christian
    Protestants
    Evangelists
    Behais
    some Jews

1

2

investigating the potential market

investigating the potential market

An outline of some of the myriad
organisations which exist to assist
the exporter, along with an
assessment of their focus and
likely relevance.

Sources of Information

Business travellers should be as well informed as possible before entering a new market. The following pages give details of some of the sources of information that are available for British and American travellers. They include details of government and private sources, reliable market and financial information and where to look on the web.

Whether you are visiting Lebanon for the first time or are making the latest of a series of regular visits, up to date intelligence and information is vital. Gathering information from various sources is also a valuable exercise in order to prevent any local bias influencing your decisions. Using the latest information will enable the business executive to use his time economically and fruitfully and avoid a lengthy learning period whilst in the country.

Do not expect to understand the country or its people immediately. Only by regular visits and the building of relationships with trusted contacts, can any executive feel confident in making sound decisions and judgements.

Official UK sources of information

The Lebanese Embassy is one obvious starting point for the business executive about to embark on a trip to Lebanon. However, the primary sources of information and advice in the UK are the British Government's Department of Trade and Industry (DTI) and the Foreign and Commonwealth Office (FCO). In addition, there are also other British Government specialist departments, e.g. the Department for Transport (DFT) [www.dft.gov.uk] and the Department for Environment, Food and Rural Affairs (DEFRA) [www.defra.gov.uk] (both of which previously came under the umbrella of the Department for the Environment, Transport and the Regions). Other sectors are equally represented by UK departments, e.g. Health, Defence, etc, and they too will have specialised people concerned with exports. The European Union also has offices in London and has representatives who can offer advice.

The DTI and FCO are probably the most important sources of information and advice. Indeed in recognition of the importance they attach to assisting UK exporters, they have formed a joint venture (JV) known as the

2

Trade Partners UK (TPUK) (formerly known as British Trade International and Overseas Trade Services). This Directorate has been charged with coordinating the commercial affairs and export promotion of the British Government overseas. It is their responsibility to ensure that industry and government have the same objectives in promoting trade. The DTI still exists and offers some services, but generally all export services come under the banner of TPUK.

Lebanese Embassy in London

Though it has very limited resources, the Embassy will give some information on tourism and useful addresses. They may refer you to the Arab British Chamber of Commerce or to the Middle East Association (see pp 36-7).

Lebanese Embassy UK
21, Palace Gardens Mews
London W8 4RA
❑ Tel: 020 7229 7265; fax 020 7243 1699

In the US and Canada, official starting points for information are also the respective embassies which can be found at the following addresses:

US
Lebanese Embassy
2560 28th Street, NW
Washington
DC 20008
❑ Tel: 202 939 6300; fax: 202 939 6324

Canada
Lebanese Embassy
640 Lyon Street,
Ottawa
Ontario, K1S 3Z5
❑ Tel: 613 236-5825,-5855; fax: 613 232-1609
E-mail: [emblebanon@synapse.net]

Official UK Sources of Information

The Department of Trade and Industry (DTI) and Trade Partners UK (TPUK)

The head office of the DTI is in Victoria Street London. Half way between Victoria Station and the Palace of Westminster is Kingsgate House, number 66-74 Victoria

Street, where the export desks for all countries are based. Other DTI offices include Number 1, Victoria Street, where the principal executives, including the Secretary of State have their offices.

Government Acronyms

The DTI as, in most government offices around the world, uses acronyms wherever possible. Indeed when an acronym cannot be concocted, the use of initial letters for departments is used – even to the extent that it may take longer to say! So it is that organisations within the DTI offer services like the late BOTB (The British Overseas Trade Board), JEPD (couldn't make an acronym from this), EMIC (easy to say), PEP (no relation to the investments), GONE (which is not self-explanatory) OSO (can be viewed in any direction and up side down) and X triple A. To the uninitiated it can be very confusing to hear civil servants talking to each other in this strange language. There is BREEZE (British Exclusive Economic Zone Export Team), IPPA (Investment Promotion and Protection Agreements), BNSC (British National Space Centre – suitably housed in a small but smart establishment in Eccleston Square, quite unlike its equivalent in the United States), NPL CQM (the National Physical Laboratory Centre for Quantum Metrology – a very popular venue) – to name but a few. And then spare a thought for that élite band of senior mandarins, the Parliamentary Under-Secretaries of State (PUSS). And somewhere within the organisation has to be a group inventing acronyms and names. For, whilst the functions of these offices generally remain, their location and their names, like the officials in them, are changing continually. And when there are no major institutional changes to be made, the furniture removal men will move offices and their contents from one floor to another within the building over a weekend – just to keep in practice. Whilst this might be seen to be difficult for DTI visitors, it is even worse for those whose desks are on the move and those who are required to keep track of their 'servants' and keep the internal telephone directory up to date.

2

Wherever the UK has done or is doing business in the world, there is a dedicated desk officer. This person is the TPUK's expert in a particular country and, most importantly, will know whom to contact within the UK government to offer the best advice. Start here and persevere! Ask about sources of further information. What is the competition? Is there a market for the product or service? Are there any restrictions on export from the UK or problems importing the product into Lebanon? Who else can give particular advice? Is there any published information available from the TPUK? (Answer – yes.) Can they suggest any contacts in Lebanon? Whilst they may not know the answers to all the questions, they will know who does.

❑ TPUK: 0207 215 5444

EMIC

One of the most useful sources of primary information at the DTI is the **Export Market Information Centre** (EMIC) – currently known as DTI XP7. EMIC provides exporters and researchers with a comprehensive library of information about a country – foreign statistics, trade directories, development plans, telephone directories and Yellow Pages (where they exist), and company profiles and catalogues. This information is available in hard copy and CD-ROM format. EMIC can be found on the Internet at [www.dti.uk/ots/emic/]. Access to the library is free and books and guides on Lebanon are available in the bookshop. In addition to the library, EMIC can carry out fee-based research, in association with the British Embassy.

❑ EMIC: 0207 215 5444 or 4351
E-mail: [EMIC@xpd3.dti.gov.uk]

Internet information is also available for those exporting companies which register with the DTI's export service Database. This service is currently free and offers overseas buyers the opportunity to contact a UK company directly and to obtain sales leads as and when they might arise. Look in [www.tradeuk.com] for information or contact the service through [export@dialog.com]. Also on the web is information about Lebanon at [www.dti.gov.uk/ots/tfairdatbase]

PEP

Projects Export Division (PEP) could be the next port of call for a would-be exporter to Lebanon. This department is responsible for major exports and projects – for example railways, airports, power, and finance. PEP also hosts the experts on the World Aid programmes. Information about proposed and existing foreign-aided projects is available on a regular basis, fed to the World Aid Section (WAS) directly from the source of aid – e.g. the European Union, the World Bank, African Development Bank, etc. This information plots the progress of a project from its inception to the point where the aid is given. This is all particularly useful for larger projects. (This information is generally only available to visitors and cannot be sent by post or given over a telephone.)

WAS

Some potential exporters may be unable to visit London and the offices suggested above. There are alternative sources of general information available. There are also regional offices that represent central government. They offer similar services to those offered by the DTI, the DETR, etc. For example, the Government Office for the North East (GONE) is one such office in Newcastle. And should Newcastle or one of the other nine GOs not be near enough, then Business Link offices exist in most major towns in the UK and are often located in or near the local chamber of commerce offices. The Northern Development Company is an example of an organisation set up in a region for the specific purpose of assisting the local unemployed. All these offices will have an individual or even a team with experience in exporting products worldwide. They can even offer companies direct assistance to develop an overseas market with the help of specialist consultants, who will work alongside the company's team.

Business Link

2

For those living north of the border, **Scottish Trade International**, in Glasgow, is a very active organisation. The Irish too are very active in the region and even have their own investment offices in Dubai.

The Oil and Gas Projects Supplies Office (OSO), with offices in London, Glasgow and Aberdeen, was set up to support the industries involved with the North Sea developments. OSO not only supports the industries in the North Sea but also tries to encourage and assist these industries to export their technology and equipment.

OSO

Another source of assistance, which is totally free, is available from **Export Promoters** (EPs), who are business

Export Promoters

35

people seconded from industry for a period of up to five years. The majority of these are experts with specialist knowledge of particular countries; in some cases they are industry specialists. Export Promoters (EPs) can be contacted by anyone. They are likely to be frequent visitors to their countries of responsibility and will have a lot of information relating to opportunities, agents, partners, exhibitions, trade missions, etc. They can generally be found through the Country Desk Officer at the DTI in Kingsgate House. These EPs are well informed and should be able to give direct, unbiased answers about their markets and whether an opportunity for a particular company might exist. Their time and assistance is free and they will usually be able to help a company with introductions and contacts at the highest level. They report directly to the Minister for Trade in the UK and overseas work closely with the Commercial section of the Embassy.

ECGD

The **Export Credits Guarantee Department** (ECGD), is also associated with the DTI, but is no longer financed by the British Government and has to be financially self-supporting. ECGD, like its European counterparts, COFACE, HERMES, etc., is loosely an overseas investment insurance scheme. The services offered by this organisation are very specialised and complicated. Essentially, they insure risk associated with any investment by a British institution or business overseas.

It is arguable that when ECGD cover is available the risk involved becomes minimal. ECGD can, however, offer customers ways to make deferred payments, which can have its attractions.

One of the most common ways in which ECGD becomes involved with an export opportunity is through a line of credit. When a UK bank offers a facility to an overseas bank to enable goods or services to be purchased from the UK, ECGD can insure that risk. The loan is used to pay the exporter once the goods have been exported or the service performed. If the borrower fails to repay any part of the loan then the UK bank is covered by the ECGD guarantee. These lines of credit can offer the overseas buyer a period of credit, whilst the exporter will get paid promptly.

Political and economic factors are regularly considered by ECGD when reviewing the availability of support.

2

❑ ECGD: 020 7512 7000
E-mail: [help@ecgd.gov.uk]
Website: [www.open.gov.uk/ecgd]

Construction

Immediately after the end of the civil conflict in
Lebanon, the DETR and its Minister for Construction
were regular visitors, together with businessmen and
women who were particularly interested in construction
and environmental issues. These groups included
lawyers, bankers, contractors, town planners,
consultants and manufacturers, all with an ambition to
assist with the reconstruction of the country. At that time
this assistance was gratefully received and many British
advisors and consultants took up opportunities in
Lebanon. The DETR was very active in promoting its
services and those of its businesses throughout the world
and was particularly active in the Middle East. The
DETR became the DTLR and lost most of its interest in
overseas markets. DTLR Department of Transport,
Local Government and the Regions – now the
Department for Transport and the Deputy Prime
Minister. However the construction baton has been
passed to the DTI/TPUK, where the same individuals
continue to support environment and the construction
industries.

DETR

Foreign and Commonwealth Office (FCO)

The FCO, situated off Whitehall in London, like TPUK
has desk officers who are concerned with events in
particular countries. In London, they are less involved
with commercial affairs, but can advise businessmen
about the political situation and can give their latest
advice concerning travel within the area. The FCO and
the Commercial Section of the British Embassy in Beirut
will have their own views of the needs of Lebanon, and
what expertise the UK may have to offer. However
reliable and accurate their information may be, there is
inevitably a niche market for almost anything, as many
entrepreneurs have proved. The FCO has also
information available via the Internet on
[www.fco.gov.uk]. This page also gives travel advice for
Lebanon – particularly important in times of unrest or
international tension.

FCO

2

British Embassy in Beirut
❑ Tel: 00961 (01) 990 400; fax: (01) 990 420
E-mail: [britemb@cyberia.net.lb]
Website: [www.britishembassy.org.lb]

US Embassy in Beirut
United States Embassy in Beirut
P.O.Box: 70-840
Antelias
Beirut
Lebanon
❑ Tel: (04) 542-600/(04) 543-600; fax: (04) 544-136
The commercial desk at the Aoucar branch of the
Embassy is particularly helpful:

Naaman Tayyar
Commercial Specialist
U.S. Embassy
Aoucar, Lebanon
❑ Tel: 961-4-544868; fax: 961-4-544794

To contact the Embassy from the United States:

United States Embassy Beirut
6070 Beirut Place, Department of State
Washington DC, 20521-6070
❑ Tel: 011 961 4 542 600/011-961 4 543 600
Fax: 011-961-4-544-136

Military Sales

Advice on sales of military equipment can be obtained
from a specialist organisation in London, the **Defence
Export Sales Organisation** (DESO) which is part of the
Ministry of Defence. They too have a very active export
service often manned by senior diplomats on secondment
to DESO for a few years. This area of business is very
specialised and, even overseas, is not handled by the
normal Commercial Officers of the Embassy but by the
Defence Attaché. Defence sales not only include obvious
military hardware and equipment but can also include the
construction of airfields, supply of 4 x 4 vehicles, supply
of uniforms to an overseas army, etc. DESO will also
advise on any political sensitivity in the region.

DESO

Education

The UK Department of Education and Employment do
not take an active part in promoting the export

2

capabilities of their associated UK industries; the **British Council** undertakes this task overseas.

The British Council has had a long relationship with Lebanon and was one of the few international cultural agencies that maintained a presence throughout the war.

The Council is responsible for cultural and educational affairs overseas. However, it is also very active in supporting UK educational and cultural industries. The Council, with offices in London, Manchester and throughout the UK, has to be self-sufficient and can no longer rely upon government subsidies. It has therefore (perhaps reluctantly at first) entered the world of commerce and trade. The Council has officers responsible for exports and also for liaison with other government bodies, in particular the DTI/TPUK.

British Council in London
❏ Tel: 0207 389 4141
Website: [www.britcoun.org]

Other British Ministries

The Departments of Health and Environment, Food and Rural Affairs in the UK also promote their exporters overseas. Both Deaprtments have export departments with their own specialised skills. As with other UK Departments, their Ministers will visit Lebanon accompanied by business executives from the relevant sectors. During these visits, sector seminars are sometimes arranged.

Department of Health: [www.doh.gov.uk]

Department for Environment, Food and Rural Affairs: [www.defra.gov.uk]

The European Union (EU)

The most important organisation of the Union concerned with business in the UK and overseas is the Directorate General 1 (DG1) dealing with trade and political matters and with offices in Brussels and overseas. (DG1 can be likened to the British FCO). DG1 controls the Mediterranean Development Aid (MEDA) programme, a substantial sum of aid and loans (currently 11bn Euro) available for selected projects in the region. DG1 also controls the **European Community Investment Partners** scheme (ECIP), and relations with the **European Investment Bank** (EIB). DG1 has country desks, much the same as the British DTI and the FCO, with desk officers, who can offer information and assistance.

ECIP

There are funds available from the Union for various development programmes apart from direct project finance. There is money available for companies to set up partnerships and/or joint ventures in Lebanon. The ECIP scheme can assist with finance to form such a joint venture and for training of personnel. ECIP can also finance feasibility studies prior to a joint venture agreement.

Further assistance and advice can be obtained from various sources such as the Commercial Section of the United Kingdom Permanent Representation (UKRep) office in Brussels, which exists to assist British companies to understand and participate in the programmes administered by European institutions in Brussels. EMIC at the DTI in London can also help. In recent years a Development Business Team in the DTI's Export Promotion Directorate was set up to assist small and medium sized enterprises (SMEs) win business through aid-funded projects and offer advice about aid funds from Europe. The Arab British Chamber of Commerce in London can also offer advice on the workings of the EU. Registration with Brussels is essential for consultants. Manufacturers with specialised products should also get pre-qualified in Brussels to participate in EU-funded projects.

Further British Sources of Information

There are a variety of organisations that can help prospective exporters to Lebanon. Trade associations, regional groups, exporters clubs, private individuals (consultants) all exist. Examples of some of these organisations are listed below. The following list is not definitive but merely indicates the types of such organisations that exist and how they might help.

The Middle East Association

The Middle East Association is an independent private organisation set up in 1961 by a group of British companies to promote trade between the UK and the Middle East. It is a non-political and non-profit making organisation financed entirely by private subscription. It works with Middle Eastern Embassies in London and with other official and semi-official bodies such as the Foreign and Commonwealth Office, the Department of Trade and Industry, the Export Credits Guarantee Department, and the Confederation of British Industry. It works with other trade associations and Chambers of Commerce and Industry in the UK and overseas. The aim of the Association is to offer its members advice on all aspects of Middle East trade and to channel to them business opportunities, introductions and enquiries from overseas. The Association has a library and information centre at its offices in Bury Street. With the support of the DTI, it sponsors overseas missions and UK participation in trade exhibitions in the Middle East.

The Association holds regular functions at its headquarters for its members, which include lunches with guest speakers from the region. Another useful event is their monthly at home, where members meet informally to discuss current events and opportunities. A fortnightly *Information Digest* is circulated to its members.

MEA
❑ Tel: 0207 839 2137
Website: [www.the-mea.co.uk]

The Arab British Chamber of Commerce
The Arab British Chamber of Commerce (ABCC), located in Belgrave Square, London, was set up in 1975 and represents all the Arab Chambers of Commerce together with British commercial interests, which include the main UK Chambers. The ABCC is responsible for mutual trade and economic interests through meetings, exhibitions and publications throughout the Middle East. A regular journal is freely available to those interested. The ABBC is also a facilitator for the European Community Investment Partners scheme (ECIP) and this office has all the details of this programme and how to access it, together with details of many of the other EU funded programmes.

ABCC
❑ Tel: 0207 235 4363
E-mail: [bims@abccbims.force9.co.uk]

American Lebanese Chamber of Commerce

This is best contacted when in Lebanon, and is efficient in providing necessary documentation and assistance.

ALCC

ALCC
1153 Foch Street
Beirut Central District
PO Box 175093
Beirut
Lebanon
❏ Tel: 961 1 985 330; fax: 961 1 985 331
Email: [AMCHAMLB@cyberia.net.lb]

Trade Associations

There is a trade association for every conceivable industry in the UK – even the Briar Pipe Trade Association. Some are large and are particularly directed to promote exports for their members – for example, the Electrical Installation Equipment Manufacturers Association Ltd, and their partners the Federation of British Electrotechnical and Allied Manufacturers Associations (BEAMA). These organisations will assist their members in taking part in trade fairs and even organise seminars and conferences to run concurrently with these events, to promote British industries. Other smaller groups such as the British Contract Furnishing Association will target particular countries where they believe the greatest opportunities exist for their members. Public and private sectors have come together to form the Export Action Centre to promote the exports of construction materials overseas – an association of the DETR export unit and the Council for Building Materials.

The list of associations is long and includes every industry, from agriculture, fisheries and food, to leisure and entertainment, and from finance and banking to clothing and fashion design.

Some associations will organise trade missions, others will organise trade fairs or help their members exhibit at international events overseas. There are bureaux, councils, federations, and societies all supporting their members and helping to promote exports. Full details of all the associations are available from **CBD Research Ltd**, in Kent, who publish a *Directory of British Associations* in hard copy or CD-ROM format. CBD can be found on the Internet on [www.glen.co.uk]. In addition, addresses and contacts at these associations can be found in local directories or through the DTI. Many of these associations have developed their own websites.

Export clubs also exist. These are informal local groups that meet occasionally to exchange experiences and ideas and to assist each other in developing their businesses. Finally, there are the private consultants and individuals who can help promote trade with Lebanon.

US Official Sources of Information

US State, Trade and Commerce Departments

The following Departments all offer assistance and advice about the respective aspects of doing business with Lebanon.

US Department Of State
Office of Business Affairs
❑ Tel: 202 647 1625; fax: 202 647 3953
Website: [www.state.gov]

U.S. Department of Commerce
Foreign Commercial Service
Lebanon Desk
❑ Tel: 202 482 1860; fax: 202 482 0878
Website: [www.ita.doc.gov]

U.S. Department Of State
Lebanon Desk (Economics)
Tel: 202 647 1058; fax:202 647 0989
E-mail: [Belldm@state.gov]

U.S. Trade and Development Agency
Middle East and North Africa Country Manager
❑ Tel: 703 875 4357; fax: 703 875 4009
E-mail: [info@tda.gov]
Website: [www.tda.gov]

Alternatively, the US Government Export Portal provides information and assistance and can be found at [www.export.gov] or 1 800 USA TRADE.

Digging Deeper

Once you have an overview of the market in Lebanon, you may want more detailed economic information or wish to concentrate on your particular sector. This is where the cost of research starts to increase – but you will

2

be very well informed and the risk of unpleasant surprises later on will be much reduced. You will be aware of the trends and the possible effects on your business and therefore able to plan for them.

Having obtained a general overview, or after a preliminary visit to Lebanon, more detailed economic or political information may be necessary. Details about local companies or agents may also be useful. The following sources will give a greater insight into the country.

Economic and country guides

Dun & Bradstreet
Holmer's Farm Way
High Wycombe
Bucks, HP12 4UL
❏ Tel: +44 1494 422000; fax: +44 1494 422260
Website: [www.dunandbrad.co.uk]

Dun & Bradstreet
899 Eaton Avenue
Bethlehem
PA 18025
USA
❏ Tel: +44 1-800 932 0025; fax: +44 1-610 882 6005

EIU (Economist Intelligence Unit)
15 Regent Street
London, SW1Y 4LR
❏ Tel: +44 20 7830 1000; fax: +44 20 7830 1023
E-mail: [london@eiu.com]
Website: [www.eiu.com]

The Economist Building
111 West 57th Street
New York, NY 10019
USA
❏ Tel: +44 1 212 554 0600; fax: +44 1 212 586 1181

MEED (Middle East Economic Digest)
21 John Street
London WC1N 2BP
❏ Tel: +44 20 7505 8000; fax: +44 20 7831 9537
Website: [www.meed.com]

Dun & Bradstreet

2

MEED

Dow Jones Reuters Business Briefing
Reuters Limited
85 Fleet Street
London
EC4P 4AJ
❑ Tel: + 44 207 542 5043

Travel Advice

The most convenient source of travel advice from the UK
is the **Foreign and Commonwealth Office** (FCO) travel
advisory service. This can be accessed either by telephone
or on-line. It provides succinct information and advice
on natural disasters, health concerns, security and
political issues. It is more than adequate for most
business travellers' needs. Be aware though that it is
aimed at a wide audience and is not geared solely
towards the business visitor's requirements.

The FCO travel advisory service can be contacted on:

❑ Tel: +44 20 7238 4503/4
Website: [www.fco.gov.uk/travel]

Or on Ceefax on BBC2 page 470

The **US State Department** advice service can be found at:
[www.state.gov/travel_warnings]. Their reports can
sometimes seem alarmist as they are legally obliged to
publish any threats to US citizens and their property of
which it is aware. Also see [www.usis.egnet.net].

For travel information and advice geared specifically
towards the business traveller's needs, you must turn to the
private sector. Here there are some good but expensive
services which provide more frequently updated reports
than the FCO or State Department travel notices. These
services tend to be more forward-looking, commenting for
instance on the likelihood of further security incidents or
the possible deterioration or improvement in the travel
environment. They are also usually more frank about a
country as they do not have the same political restraints as
the FCO or State Department.

Keeping Up to Date

Publications

After you have thoroughly researched the market and
started operations in the country, it is essential to keep

2

up-to-date about developments both in your particular sector and in the wider market.

The easiest way is to monitor the press and media for stories on Lebanon. The country receives adequate coverage in the international press and most British newspapers and news organisations have correspondents based in the region. The internet editions of some newspapers and media organisations offer news e-mail services, which send stories on specified subjects to your e-mail address.

Others allow you to produce customised pages, which are updated with stories on your chosen subjects. One of the best is CNN's service (see [cnn.com]).

The Internet

In a spare moment before departure, whilst pondering Lebanon, it would be well worth browsing through the internet for general information about the country. Surfing the web will bring up a variety of organisations and information sources. In particular the following sites may be worth looking at:

L'Orient-Le Jour:
[www.lorientlejour.com]

Le Commerce du Levant:
[www.lecommercedulevant.com]

Daily Star:
[www.thedailystar.com.lb]

Lebanon Opportunities:
[www.infopro.com] or [www.lebanonopportunities.com]

Directory, Yellow Pages:
[www.yellowpages.com.lb]

Association of Lebanese Industrialists:
[www.ali.org.lb]

The Beirut Chamber of Commerce & Industry:
[www.euroinfocentre.net]

IDAL: Investment Development Authority of Lebanon:
[www.idal.com]

Bankers' Association:
[www.abl.org.lb]

2

Croner is a leading publisher of loose-leaf, regularly updated guidance on international trade. Their comprehensive Reference Book for Exporters concentrates on the practicalities of import and export procedures for over 170 countries, and explains both UK and foreign government regulations and restrictions in detail. In addition, Croner's website, tradeinternational-centre.net, is a good place to find free Country information, and register for free e-newsletters on your areas of interest. 2002 also saw the re-launch of a monthly subscription magazine Trade International Digest.

Croner
145 London Road
Kingston upon Thames
Surrey
KT2 6SR
❑ Tel: +44 20 8547 3333; fax: +44 20 8547 2638
Website: [www.tradeinternational-centre.net]

2

3

getting to Lebanon

getting to Lebanon

3

Various considerations in
arranging travel to Lebanon.

The tourist industry is now offering package tours to Lebanon. However, the business traveller will have different criteria and concerns. Is the location of a hotel suitable? Are flights convenient and, these days a question that is more often asked, is it good value? The business visitor will need to make careful arrangements before he/she leaves for Lebanon in order to make the best use of his/her time.

Trade Missions

One option is to join one of the many regular missions going to the country; this is especially suitable for the first-time visitor to Lebanon. There are many associations who organise such missions. One immediate advantage of joining such a group is that they will organise flights, hotels, transport, visas, etc, for the delegates, and in many cases will have government financial support for the trip. These groups, especially those that might accompany a British official (for instance, Government Minister), will also have a programme of events organised for them, including meetings with Lebanese officials and senior businessmen, dinners and other social/business events. Ministerial missions will usually have a pre-departure briefing in the UK and a debriefing some months later, to establish aims and to report back on successes or otherwise.

Someone from the organising body will usually accompany trade missions. This person will be responsible for ensuring that the group is in the right place at the right time. They will make sure that hotel transfers go according to plan and that any individual requirements are sorted out. They will reconfirm flights and transport arrangements. They will often know who the delegates should contact and how to get around town. They will be able to advise on etiquette and will know who to contact if there are any problems arising. All very comforting for a first-time visitor, and the interaction between the mission members will be a great asset.

Visas

Visas are required to enter Lebanon. They can be bought in London at the Lebanese Embassy or on arrival at the airport. The rates for these visas in London vary

3

according to the duration of stay, whether the visa is for tourism or business and whether it is a single or multiple-entry visa. The visa purchased at Beirut airport costs $15 and is valid only for one visit of less than a month. It is usually safer to obtain the visa before travel.

Make sure that you have no Israeli visa in your passport!

In the USA, Lebanese visas can be bought from Lebanese Consulates in Northampton or L.A. or Levon Travel Headquarters:

1132 N. Brand Blvd
Glendale
California 91202
❏ Tel: 800 445 3866; fax: 818 552 7701
Email: [sales@levontravel.com]

Airport

Beirut has a new airport, which was opened in 2000. It replaces the old one, which had survived attacks and occupation during the war. The new buildings and runway are modern and offer excellent facilities for travellers.

The need for a new terminal was first recognised in the 1960s and construction started and stopped on several occasions during lulls in the war. Remnants of the contractors' efforts could be seen until work on the new facility was started, and crates with new air-bridge equipment lay on the tarmac rusting away for decades. Runways and taxiways were pockmarked by tank tracks and repaired shell holes.

The old airport, although crowded and damaged during the conflict, remained efficient in transferring a traveller from plane to taxi – usually in about 15 minutes. Despite the ancient tractors and luggage-conveying equipment including one old luggage carrousel, airport staff were as efficient as anywhere in the world. They still are.

The new terminal offers the best service and facilities in the region.

3

Travel to Beirut

Most international flights to Lebanon arrive in Beirut. There are frequent flights operated by most European and Middle Eastern carriers. Middle East Airlines, the flag carrier of Lebanon, is a reasonable airline which offers a good alternative to many of the European airlines and is keen to offer a good service.

There are few alternatives for travel to Lebanon. There are now no passenger railways in the country. The old narrow gauge railway to Damascus across the mountains ceased operation many years ago, and the coastal railway to the north and Tripoli stopped operations in the 1990s. For the enthusiast, remnants of both these systems can be seen at various locations. Plans for a rail-link north and south are a long way off.

There is a limited ferry service to Cyprus from Jounieh. This sea crossing was, during particularly difficult times of the war, the only way of entering the country and was used by the Lebanese.

The road from Damascus to Beirut, across the mountains and through the Bekaa Valley, is an easy route between Lebanon and Syria. Special taxis are available from Beirut, but these can only take passengers to the taxi terminal and not to hotels in Damascus or anywhere else. Remember that a visa for Syria must be obtained *before* arrival in Lebanon.

Hotels

Hotels should be booked before departure, especially if a particular hotel or location is essential. Despite many misconceptions about Lebanon, its hotels can get very full at times for no obvious reason. All hotels, large or small, offer excellent service and accommodation.

Many hotels will offer (for a fee) to meet the traveller at the airport and transport them to their hotel. This service is a comfort to any traveller, especially those new to Lebanon.

Money

Lebanon now has a reasonably stable exchange rate. The local currency, the Lebanese pound, is not readily available offshore. Travellers should take US dollars, which are still widely accepted throughout the country –

3

during difficult times and fluctuating foreign exchange rates, countries seem to fall back on the dollar.

Credit cards are acceptable everywhere and ATMs can be found at most banks – of which there are many.

Personal cheques are accepted in certain exchange outlets e.g. American Express, although suitable identification will be required.

Health

There are now good health services in Lebanon, and BUPA-registered hospitals. Generally hygiene is good and few problems should be encountered with food and drinking water.

Doctors and health clinics will advise on inoculations that may be required before arriving and local GPs or even airlines offer medical services and advice to travellers.

Travel Insurance

Most travellers are covered either through their own company medical schemes or through the prudent use of credit cards to pay for airfares. Travel agents will offer full cover against illness or loss of possessions.

Planned Meetings before Departure

It is advisable for any executive travelling to Lebanon to arrange some core meetings before arrival. The commercial section of the Embassy in Beirut is always a good place to start. Embassy staff will help direct the newcomer and advise the old hands on the current political, economical and commercial state of the country. The British Embassy's current office, in Jal el-Dib is quite convenient for the centre of town.

Some companies will have had a sector survey carried out by the Embassy before their departure. They will probably have had a list of names that they might consider contacting before arrival in Beirut.

Making the Embassy aware that you are in the country is useful from the point of view of personal security, especially in times of political instability in the region.

There is a **British Businessmen's Group** that meets regularly. The time and place of meetings can be found out from the British Embassy Commercial section. (see chapter 5, pp65-6 for details)

It is not necessary to arrange a full programme of events before departure. Indeed, as we shall see, it would be most unwise – time should be allowed for the unexpected. Traffic conditions in Beirut are the first obvious restriction on the number of meetings one can attend in a day.

It is unwise to commit oneself to any organisation or individual before the market is thoroughly explored and understood – despite possible glowing letters of introduction. It is advisable to retain full independence on the first visit, until one is happy with a local associate (if one is required).

For details of American Lebanese Business groups, contact:

Arab-American Business Association
P.O. Box 753
Huntington Beach, Ca. 92648
❏ Tel: 714 893-0121
Fax 714 893-0083
Website: [www.ArabAmericanBusiness.com]

AABA

3

What to Take

Apart from the usual travel documents, little else need be taken except for business documents and literature. Many businessmen take laptop computers – short-term links to a local ISP in Lebanon are possible. GSM mobile phones work in most of the country. Cameras are allowed.

An international driving licence is required to drive in Lebanon, which can be obtained from driving organisations in the UK or US.

It is wise to take a supply of any medication you regularly require.

4

the ground rules

the ground rules

This section takes the reader by
the hand and talks through the
nitty-gritty of everyday life,
from how to get around to how
much to tip the bell-boy.

Travellers to Lebanon arrive in the new Beirut Airport. The calm and efficiency of the terminal will no doubt impress, and assuage any anxieties about coming to Lebanon. The rapid transfer from airport to hotel will equally impress the executive.

Whilst the majority of business in Lebanon revolves around Beirut, there are major industrial centres in Tripoli, along the coast between these two cities and to the south. Most businesses, ministries and prospective clients will have their offices in Beirut, although there is an increasing trend for offices to move out of the centre to the suburbs. When the new Beirut Central District (BCD) is finally complete, it is probable that more and more businesses and institutions will return to the heart of the city.

How then do business travellers conduct themselves and what precautions should they take? Is Beirut really so confusing? Over the next few pages some of the myths and difficulties will be explained to enable the business executive to travel in comfort and make the most of the visit.

4

Personal Finances

Cash can be brought in to Lebanon in reasonable amounts with no restrictions on currency. When it comes to money and persuading customers to part with their money, the Lebanese are second to none, and can make it seem painless!

Cash and Lebanese currency

The local currency is the Lebanese pound or Lira, denoted by LL. The pound is theoretically allowed by the Central Bank to float freely and has remained stable against the US dollar for many years. It fluctuates slightly against other currencies as a result of changes in the international value of the dollar. 1500 Lebanese pounds (LL1500) is approximately equivalent to 1 US dollar and LL2300 equivalent to 1pound sterling (2002).

Money

The Lebanese currency is generally in paper notes, with an occasional coin still around. Notes available are LL100, 250, 500, 1,000, 5,000, 10,000, 20,000, 50,000 and 100,000 denominations.

Payments for most things will be in local currency or in US dollars. Hotels may advertise their room rates in US dollars, but these days will usually take any currency. Although the Lebanese pound is freely exchangeable anywhere, it is still difficult to obtain Lebanese pounds outside Lebanon.

Dollars are still used anywhere and other currencies such as Stirling and Euros are readily exchangeable.

Banks and Exchanges

There are over 60 licensed banks in Lebanon, of which 14 are foreign.

Money

Currency exchange desks exist in most hotels, certainly the large ones. It is possible to get the hotel to change money through their own cashiers, if the formal exchange banks are closed. You will find many exchanges in the major streets, and Lebanese bureaux banks are consumer friendly and will exchange most currencies in and out of the Lebanese pounds.

4

On the wider issues of personal banking, there are two British Banks represented in Beirut; HSBC (formerly the British Bank of the Middle East) and Standard Chartered. There are also associated investment banks, e.g. British Arab Commercial Bank (BACB which used to be UBAF). It is unlikely that the business executive or traveller will have any short-term need for personal banking services.

Other foreign banks are Citibank, Banco Di Roma, BNP, Société Générale and many Arab banks such as NBK, Arab Bank, ABC, etc.

Transport

Most business travellers to Lebanon are likely to travel around by road, either by taxi or hired car.

Cars

Lebanon operates a 'service' taxi system. This means that a taxi will pick up passengers throughout its journey. Western travellers should not be surprised if they find their taxi stopping to pick up additional passengers.

Taxis

Taxis have metres, which, by law, should work! The wearing of seat belts is compulsory. It is advisable before getting into a taxi, especially one of the taxis waiting outside hotels, to negotiate a price for a journey. Taxis from hotels are generally more expensive than one hailed in the street, but are usually cleaner and more mechanically sound.

It can be difficult to distinguish a taxi from any other car, although many now have a Taxi sign. They are generally middle-aged Mercedes cars with drivers. The best way to recognise a taxi is by its red number plate.

A useful tip for business travellers when taking a taxi from a hotel is to negotiate a daily or half-daily rate. Drivers will be more than happy to come to some such arrangement. They will wait while their passengers have a meeting, then carry on to another meeting or return to the hotel. If required to wait they are usually quite trusting and will not expect to get paid until the end of the journey. It can be very difficult to find empty taxis on the street, so this system is best.

Buses
Business travellers are unlikely to travel in a public bus even if they could identify one! There is, however, a bus service within Beirut and to Tripoli in the north and Aleppo, Damascus, and Latakia in Syria.

Trains
Sadly no more – the remnants can be seen at the engine shed in Tripoli.

Private or Hired Car
Most hotels will be able to arrange a private car for hire with or without a driver. As parking, and indeed driving, in Beirut and beyond is extremely difficult, chauffeur-driven hire cars make it easier to carry out a programme of meetings. It will of course be more expensive than and easier than taxis but perhaps more reassuring.

Boats
The 'beautiful people' of Lebanon can be seen at the various marinas and desporting themselves on boats at the weekend up and down the coast – as a mode of business travel this is an unlikely option.

Communications
After the war, the telephone system in Lebanon was in chaos. Few lines existed and those that did were likely to be illegal or at least have an illegal connection. To the

4

Lebanese, who had relied on efficient communications, rebuilding the country's communications infrastructure was a priority. The system now is one of the most modern in the region with access readily available for anyone.

Mobile phones were introduced into the country very soon after the war. Two networks soon covered the whole of the country, even in the mountains. Hotels will arrange the hire of a cellular phone if required.

> ### Mobile Phones
>
> The Lebanese took to mobile phones like the proverbial ducks to water. Just after their introduction, it was common for people to have two phones connected to the two systems. Restaurants would supply phone holders to attach to the edge of the table so that phones would not take up valuable table space. It seemed also that sun worshippers at the various exclusive swimming pools could be seen talking to each other across the sundeck – so much easier than getting up off the sun bed!
>
> This modern technology did not meet with everyone's approval however. The telephone entrepreneurs, who might have located a 'live' international line in some junction box, would lose their livelihood from the sale of international calls.
>
> Municipal purists however did rejoice in the removal of the spaghetti-like conglomeration of wires, which could be seen at the tops of telegraph poles, from which again temporary services (probably illegal) had been obtained by local residents.

Local Business Etiquette

Business in Lebanon is conducted in a relatively straightforward manner. There are generally no specific pitfalls for the business executive; no sheep's eyes, no sitting cross-legged on the floor, no bowing, etc. Lebanese have recently become used to being prompt for appointments. In the past and before the advent of mobile phones, the excuse of 'terrible traffic' was frequently used. This reason for a delayed appointment is not so widely accepted nowadays.

Before starting a meeting, coffee or tea will be offered. Coffee (*owher* or *ghower*) is usually understood to be Turkish coffee and is more likely to be served in more important offices. There will usually be a glass of water provided with the coffee, although in a big meeting there may not be one each. The water nowadays is generally bottled and safe to drink. Tea is likely to be served without milk, with a lot of sugar and in a small glass. These days it is also likely to be made with a tea bag, which will still be in place, and the problem arises of how to dispose of the bag. (Having wrung out the tea bag it can then be deposited into a saucer or empty ashtray.) Instant coffee generally known as 'Nescafé' is now increasingly offered. Other drinks that may be offered are Coke, lemonade or 7-Up or something similar.

Meetings will usually start, as in most countries, with a few pleasantries and a handshake. In Europe and America our handshakes tend to be a little perfunctory. In the Middle East, when shaking hands do not be in a hurry to withdraw your hand and even be prepared to hold hands for a little while. Introductory topics of conversation can be the traffic problems or English football – both quite acceptable. During this time the tea boy will take orders. Once the meeting has started, it is probable that the tea boy will reappear with the orders and so disrupt the meeting. The telephone too is likely to ring throughout a meeting and disturbances will inevitably come from the ubiquitous mobile phone. However, the younger and more considerate executives, and especially those who have had dealings with Western companies, will avoid unnecessary interruptions.

There is no special dress code for business meetings other than the obvious conventions of being smartly and modestly dressed. Suits for men are more usual, especially for important executives, although a blazer would be acceptable. It is discourteous to arrive in shirt sleeves only. Female executives should take more care with their attire for meetings, with at least half-length sleeves covering arms and reasonably long skirts; trousers are acceptable.

Pleasantries

4

Communal (*majlis*) meetings, where the prominent person conducts several meetings at the same time, are not as common in Lebanon as in other parts of the Middle East. Interruptions are still likely to occur, with people arriving and departing throughout, although serious business meetings would be conducted in private. It is possible that a warm-up act may be employed to welcome the visitors and to get the pleasantries out of the way allowing the 'great man' to arrive with the maximum impact when everyone else is settled.

Receptions (often arranged for visiting groups or missions) last for about two hours and while requiring formal dress are fairly relaxed and useful occasions. Alcohol will always be served. Formal dinners and luncheons often start later than advised but tend to finish promptly when the guest of honour will rise and depart, followed by the rest of the guests. No special formalities are observed, although there will probably be a top table to which dignitaries will be invited. Be prepared for vast meals with an obligatory *mezze* as an appetiser, after which at least one main course will arrive, usually followed by fresh fruit!

Religious etiquette

There are few issues in Lebanon concerned with religion that any Western traveller will become involved with. The Holy Month of Ramadan is observed by the Muslims, and Christians may also observe times of Lent and Advent. Courtesy and consideration, as ever, will prevent you from giving offence.

Tipping

This is an issue that concerns everybody. Even though restaurants will add a service charge, tips are expected. How much should we tip? Up to 10 per cent depending on satisfaction of service.

Serious tipping can be considered as follows:

At the airport:	US $2 per case
Parking the car:	$2-3
In the five-star hotel:	$5
Fast food or general deliverers:	$2
Toilet attendants:	$1
Taxis from the street:	none
A hired car with a driver:	$10 per day

Public holidays

These consist of a variety of political and religious festivals. In addition to the Christian holidays, Muslims (and others) will expect to take their religious holidays. These Islamic holidays vary from year to year and reflect the different (*hejira*) calendar used throughout the Islamic world.

General Holidays:

New Years Day	1 January
Feast of Mar Maroun	9 February
Easter	As in Europe and US
Eastern Easter	As to Greece or Russia
Qana Day	18 April
Labour Day	1 May
Martyrs Day	6 May
Assumption Day	15 August
All Saints Day	1 November
Independence Day	22 November
Christmas Day	25 December

Islamic Holidays:

Annual Festival   Approximate Dates

	2002	2003	2004	2005
Muslim New year.	15 Mar	4 Mar	22 Feb	11 Feb
Prophets Birthday	23 May	12 May	1 May	20 April
Ramadan begins	5 Nov	25 Oct	14 Oct	3 Oct
Eid al Fitr	5 Dec	24 Nov	13 Nov	2 Nov
Eid al Adha	12 Feb	1 Feb	21 Jan	10 Jan

These religious holidays can change slightly since they depend on the sighting of the moon.

4

Weather

The weather in Lebanon is like that of Southern European or the Mediterranean. Although generally pleasantly hot in the summer, it rains occasionally. In the winter, the weather is variable, with rain, snow, sun and fog.

	June – September	November - March
Rainfall		
	Nil	20-30 cms
Temperatures		
	20 - 30 degrees C	0 – 10 degrees C
Humidity		

Generally low, but higher near the sea. Relative humidity of 60-70 per cent is to be expected.

4

getting down to business

5

getting down to business

This chapter provides elementary
guidance on the basic etiquette of
business, and also contains details of
useful local organisations who can
assist with the more complicated
requirements of business transactions.

The following sources of information will assist the executive to venture into Lebanon with confidence and to develop their business.

Agents and Local Partners

Before they arrive in Lebanon many business travellers will have some ideas about the local arrangements they wish to adopt. They may indeed have a local agent or someone in mind. Companies should, of course, choose their local partner with care. It is easy to make a hasty appointment, and the difficulties of parting company with a local agent are enormous, with the benefit of the doubt always given to the local party.

There are still local businessmen who will act as an intermediary between an exporter or contractor and a possible client in order to make sure that the correct people are influenced and that they receive favourable treatment. As tenders and operations become more transparent, and indeed while this perception of transparency exists, the need for such go-betweens or fixers is less obvious. Be prepared to go it lone and sink or swim with your product or service.

There is no compulsory requirement for a local agent or partner. You can set up your own company or office and, except for banks and real estate, there is no prior requirement and no distinction between Lebanese and foreigners. New banks, foreign or local, need a Central Bank license. Real estate can be bought by non-Lebanese, but there are limitations depending on size of the property and location – check with a local lawyer or an established estate agent.

Sometimes circumstances dictate that an association should be formed with a Lebanese company. Precise specification for an open tender may indicate that the client is after a particular product. This is fine, if you happen to be the lucky company that supplies this item. Indeed it is sometimes possible to ensure that the client and his consultant are so impressed by certain equipment that either he will specify it directly or will write a specification that only one manufacturer can comply with. Product selection by specification is not uncommon and is particularly relevant where a client wants a certain item but the rules of tendering of a government, bank or other loan agency prevent the use of preferential

5

suppliers. American and European aid agencies are particularly strict with their rules for loans and grants.

You may have come to Beirut with a specific goal in mind, and need to make a presentation to a local consultant or government office. When making presentations it is worth remembering that many Lebanese offices and officials are very advanced technologically. CD-ROM-driven presentations can easily be made and may make the greatest impact, although it is advisable to check that viewing and projection equipment is available and compatible.

You may be making your first trip with an open mind. It is possible that a list of prospective agents will have been drawnup and that one or all of them will have been contacted. It is equally possible that if they have been contacted, the keener and more ambitious agent will have ensured that he was at the airport to meet and greet his possible source of income. It is not unlikely, however, that local agents endeavour to include all possible competition in their portfolio of agreements so that they can monopolise the supply of a product onto the market.

Choosing a Local Partner

5

Advice is readily available once in the country and although one source may offer suggestions and another offer a totally opposite point of view, the seasoned business traveller should be able to gather enough information from different sources to come to his own sensible conclusion. Advice about agents will obviously be a priority for a newcomer and some of these sources of information are given below. These same sources can also offer the latest information about the particular market.

Sources of statistical information are numerous but be cautious about the reliability and validity of such information. For example, official government statistics are often several months out of date, whereas unofficial sources can often give a more accurate and up-to-the-minute assessment. Local and international political events which would not be reflected in any current statistics can also affect the business. Sometimes restrictions are imposed by the government to protect the financial stability of the country and its industries. Such protection may include the imposition of import tariffs, or controls on raising letters of credit, for example.

British Embassy

Most countries have a Commercial Section to their Embassy, generally the most active section in any embassy. The British Embassy is no exception and the Commercial Section, in conjunction with British Trade International in London, is able to offer a co-ordinated service under the name of Trade Partners UK. These days, some of the more time-consuming services and written advice has to be paid for. However, most commercial officers are pleased to see any newcomer to the country and keep in touch with companies with the latest news and progress of their projects. Don't leave Lebanon without a visit to the Embassy – one day you may need their help.

The Commercial Section in the British Embassy in Beirut usually has at least one expatriate member of staff. They will be drawn from the Foreign and Commonwealth Office or the Department of Trade and Industry and will be posted to Lebanon for about three years. They are experienced in commercial work and will have a good knowledge of the local markets and, most importantly, know local sources of information that could assist any business working in Lebanon. These sources range from lawyers or accountants to agents and suppliers. They will also know the government offices and agencies. (They can also help with names of local dentists and doctors in the case of emergencies.)

In addition to the expatriate staff, there is a core of local staff who work in the Embassy on a full-time basis. They know Lebanon best and can be a good source of local information and gossip. It is these staff who assisted in preparing market reports.

The commercial section also meets the local expatriate business community on a regular basis and usually arrange lunches and informal meetings. Visitors are always welcome if they are introduced by the Embassy or local expatriates.

Contact the British Embassy Commercial Section in Central Beirut:

❏ Tel: (01) 990 400; fax: (01) 990 420
E-mail: [britemb@cyberia.net.lb]

5

Businessman's Group

Web pages for companies in the UK:
[www.britishembassy.org.lb]

For events: [www.tradeuk.com]

EU

Britons and nationals of other European countries have another source of commercial help – the Commission of the European Community in Beirut. While it is not an Embassy strictly (for example there are no facilities for issuing visas or passports), their office is a major source of aid and funds from members of the European Community and they can offer advice.

Contact the EU on:

❑ Tel: (01) 203818 ext 402/3/4/5

British Lebanese Business Association (BLBA)
❑ Tel: (04) 715900/1/2 (at the British Embassy)

Other Local organisations

Association of Lebanese Industrialists

This is the institution that brings together most major industrialists. Together with the Beirut Chamber of Commerce & Industry and the Bankers' Association, they represent the private sector in its dealings with the government.

❑ Tel: (01) 350 280-1-2; fax: (01) 351 167
E-Mail: [ali@ali.org.lb]
Website: [www.ali.org.lb]

The Beirut Chamber of Commerce & Industry

Lebanese Chambers of Commerce

An active and helpful organisation especially if you are introduced by Embassy or prominent member.

❑ Tel: (01) 353 390-1-2; fax: (01) 353 395
Website: [www.euroinfocentre.net]

There is a Data Center, which offer to business enterprises the following services:

Supplying information
Enhancing local and international profiles of enterprises
Providing services related to networks
Acting as a matchmaker in the quest for partners.

❑ Tel: 01 744 163-4/ 349 614; fax: 01 349 615
E-mail: [info@ccib.org.lb]
Website: [www.ccib.org.lb]

5

There is also a Euro Info Correspondence Centre at the Chamber of Commerce & Industry Building, which fulfils two main functions, namely:

A first-stop-shop in the provision of economic, investment and trade information; and an organizer of events and workshops.

Tel: 01 744 163-4/ 349 614; fax: 01 349 615
E-Mail: [eicc@ccib.org.lb]
Website: [www.ccib.org.lb]

The Tripoli, Saida and Zahlé Chamber of Commerce & Industry

Tripoli:
❑ Tel: (06) 432 790; fax: (06) 442 042

Saida:
❑ Tel: (07) 720 123; fax: (07) 722 986

Zahlé:
❑ Tel: (08) 817 681; fax: (08) 800 050

Other business groups in Lebanon:

Bankers' Association
All banks are members of the Bankers' Association and the Association provides useful economic and financial information on a regular basis, worth a visit.

❑ Tel: (01) 970 500; fax: (01) 970 501
E-Mail: [abl@abl.org.lb]
Website: [www.abl.org.lb]

RDCL: Rassemblement des Chefs d'Entreprise
A relatively new association of young chief executive private sector companies across the board.

❑ Tel: (01) 320 450; fax: (01) 320 395

Beirut Merchant Association
(Associasn de Commerat, de Berouth) Represents local Beirut trading companies.

Rotary Clubs
There are many Rotary Clubs in Lebanon. These groups of businessmen meet regularly and will always welcome visits from fellow Rotarians from around the world. They also support local charities through successful fund raising activities. There are also many Lions Clubs which welcome visits by fellow Lions.

5

Bankers' Association

British Council

British Council

The British Council is located in Sidani Street, Beirut. The Council maintained its presence in West Beirut throughout the war and because of this has a special position in Lebanon. It has lending and reference libraries, and a library of videos and cassettes. Information is available about the UK via its internet services, together with a large selection of directories and information available on computers or as hard copy. International newspapers and magazines are also available.

The Council runs courses for Lebanese to learn English and for foreigners to learn Arabic. Companies can use the services of the Council to run training programmes in English and other business skills. Training can also be offered on a contract basis. They can also assist in arranging places at British universities and schools and have all the up-to-date information about educational establishments in the UK.

Contact the British Council on:

❑ Tel: (01) 740 123/4/5
E-mail: [informationcentre.enquiries@lb.britishcouncil.org]

5

United Nations Agencies

UN

Like many Middle Eastern countries there is a large UN presence, ranging from aid for refugees to military peace-keeping in South Lebanon. Offices for IMF, UNICEF, UNDP, UNWRA, IFC, FAO, WHO and ILO are all located in Beirut. ESCWA: United Nation's Economic and Social Commision for Western Asia promote economic and social development through regional and subregional cooperation and integration. They also serve as the main general economic and social development forum within the United Nations system for the ESCWA region.

As with the European Union it is necessary to register products, interests and skills with most UN agencies. They can then call for a particular product from companies or consultants who have pre-qualified.

Ministries and Government Offices

The major ministries are all located in Beirut. These offices have varying amounts of information concerning Lebanon. The Ministry of Tourism, for example, can offer a lot of helpful information for tourists, while the Ministries of Economy and Planning can offer statistical information about the country together with details of current opportunities.

Government laws, especially those relating to foreign companies and their operations can be obtained from IDAL and the relevant ministries. The Chamber of Commerce in Beirut can also provide information.

IDAL: Investment Development Authority of Lebanon
IDAL is a one-stop shop for information on investment opportunities and laws. Certainly worth a visit or a browse on their web site.

IDAL

Website: [www.idal.com.lb]

Council for Development and Reconstruction (usually known as CDR):
This is directly linked to the Prime Minister's office and is responsible for the planning of major infrastructure projects. It is physically close to the Premiership Office and although its personnel has recently been reduced, it still plans and oversees major public projects.

CDR

5

Solidere:
The company that owns Beirut Central District (BCD) is the largest public company in Lebanon. It was set up to clear up and rebuild the district and since its inception in 1992 has refurbished a major part of the damaged buildings and streets in the central district and has developed a large residential and office complex. It is worth a visit to their planning office.

Solidere

Building 149 Saad Zaghoul St
Beirut 2012 7305
❏ Tel: (01) 980 650/60; fax: (01) 980 661/2
E-mail: [solidere@solidere.com.lb]
Website: [www.solidere-online.com]

Office for Statistics:
There is a Central Statistical Office, which is government controlled. Statistics relating to import-export are better obtained from relevant authorities – banking statistics from the Bankers' Association, industrial statistics from the Association of Lebanese Industrialists, trade from the Chamber of Commerce, etc.

Shipping

Shipping Agents

Laws applying to import and export change regularly. Whilst the government does not necessarily introduce new laws, old ones are sometimes resurrected and enforced, irregularities are straightened out and, or loopholes are closed to suit the circumstances.

However, there are many good shipping agents in Lebanon. Most have offices in Beirut and may have additional offices in Tripoli and Sidon. The larger Lebanese agents may also have offices or associates overseas and some will be able to consolidate shipments from overseas to Lebanon, offering a door-to-door service.

It is recommended that the newcomer to the market should use a well-known agent in Lebanon to handle all shipments both in and out of the country. Advice on specific agents can be given by Embassies or trade organisations and by talking to local businessmen. The temptation to embark upon an association with one of the smaller companies, which might offer better rates, should be viewed with caution. In the long run, the straightforward and standard approach to importation is probably the cheapest.

5

The Port of Beirut

The Port of Beirut is probably one of the most efficient ports in the region. Despite its small size, or perhaps because of it, the port authorities ensure a very rapid transfer of cargo. The port basin is a dangerous place, with unexploded ordnance lying on the silty bottom. Just after the end of the conflict, it was common to see convoys of lorries waiting to take cargo to Syria, Jordan, Turkey and beyond, and the role of the businessmen euphemistically in 'Import-Export' became clear. In the early days the port authorities used anything to remove the cargo from the ships holds and the 'forest' of old crane jibs day and night became a familiar sight. Nowadays more modern equipment is used as the new port facilities are developed.

Banking, guarantees and letters of credit

There are many banks in Lebanon – over sixty different ones at the last count. Many foreign banks will have a corresponding bank, even if they do not have their own branch. Some international banks have their own resident expatriate staff. The bank's staff will all be able to give sound advice relating to their services and the local market.

Re-Emerging Financial Centre

Before 1975 Beirut was the centre of finance in the Middle East. Since the end of the civil war in 1990, the sector has gradually reaffirmed itself locally as the driving force behind business regeneration, and has been the most profitable activity. There are 14 foreign banks, American, European, Arab and Asian, but the ten largest banks are Lebanese or part-Lebanese owned.

5

6

major industries

major industries

An overview of each of the
major industries of the nation
and where they stand.

Regeneration of Lebanon

Lebanon emerged from the war in the early 1990s and within a few years had embarked upon a major programme to reconstruct its social and urban infrastructure. After tourism, the industrial sector had suffered the most. Many factories were destroyed and have not been rebuilt.

International consultants, planners, designers, architects, industrialists and academics were recruited to regenerate the country. Many Lebanese were amongst these specialists drawn from major organisations around the world. The local community too became involved with the programme, with past differences put aside to confront the new challenge.

Lebanon is a small country with a small population, but its heritage of trading since Phoenician times ensures that international exporters should have an interest.

Economic and Social Indicators

6

	2002
Area:	10,400 sq kms
Population (m)	3.6 m
Labour force (m)	1.3 m
Annual average population growth rate:	
	1.4 per cent
Life expectancy:	71 years
Literacy:	86.4 per cent
Electricity consumption (kwh):	7.86 billion
Main telephone lines:	700,000
Unemployment (%):	18 per cent
Radio broadcast stations:	AM 20 & FM 40
Television broadcast stations:	8
Internet Service Providers (ISP):	22
Inflation (%):	under 2 per cent
Central Bank foreign exchange reserves:	
	$8.5 billion
GDP growth (%):	2 per cent

Lebanon is keen to increase exports, and has organisations at home and abroad to encourage this. In recent years, international buyers have returned to purchase products and establish permanent lines of supply. Which, American import quotas restrict the freedom of US companies to carry out such trade,lebanon has just recently signed an association agreement with the EU which allows Lebanon goods freely into the EU.

The major industries in the country are banking, tourism, food processing, jewellery, cement, textiles, mineral and chemical products, wood and furniture products, and metal fabrication.

Banking

Banking is one of Lebanon's most successful industries contributing more than 8 per cent of the national GDP .

Up until early in the 20th Century, the banking sector was only present in the Lebanon through exchange offices. It was the growth of the silk industry and the exports to France that finally prompted the setting up the first bank, a branch of the Ottoman Bank, followed shortly by the establishment of Crédit Lyonnais. Since the 1920s the banking sector has grown steadily.

In 1963 the Banque du Liban, the Republic's Central Bank, was established with the primary role of regulating the domestic banking industry and issuing the Lebanese currency, something that had, until then, had been the responsibility of the privately owned Banque de Syrie et du Liban. Through its monetary policy, and in close cooperation with the Government, the Bank endeavours to create a sound environment for economic and social progress.

Today Lebanon has 63 banks, active mostly in trade finance but also in project finance and private banking. The Central Bank has been keen to see consolidation in the banking industry and, by ensuring that the law favours the acquiring bank, some twenty-one banks have been merged with larger onesin recent years. Foreign banks wishing to set up a branch in the country (e.g. Citibank and the National Bank of Canada which opened recently) are limited to one branch only with the exception of BNP (France) and HSBC (formerly British

6

Bank of the Middle East) which are permitted to operate a number of branches in recognition of their support in carrying on business throughout the war years. For those wishing to have more branches, such as the Standard Chartered Bank, buying a majority share in an existinglocal bank, is the route to adopt.

One of the major appeals for investors and depositors in the Lebanese banking system is the banking secrecy law of September 1956, one of the toughest in the world.. Recently and in response to international concern on money laundering the Central Bank has, in cooperation with the Government, formed an independent Investigation Committee with extended prerogatives, such the forced lifting of banking secrecy on suspected accounts, and a task to investigate money-laundering operations and to monitor compliance with the rules and procedures of the law. As a result, Lebanon has now been placed on the list of approved banking nations.

Foreign currencies, mainly the US Dollar, are often used in day to day to life because of their relatively large proportion in total deposits (69.3% in December 2002) This is largely the result of high inflation and a rapid depreciation of the Lebanese Pound in the period 1978-1992. Monetary policy has since been focused on stabilising the exchange rate and controlling inflation and monetary growth.

Banking

6

The Link to the Greenback

Two thirds of banking deposits are in foreign currency and of these the majority are in US dollars. Although a large proportion of Lebanese business is with Europe, there are no current plans to equate the Lebanese currency to the Euro, and the secrecy laws of Lebanese banking make it unlikely that there will be any enthusiasm for such a move in future.

Some $51 billion are deposited in banks in Lebanon – a relatively high per capita figure Paris II, an economic summit held in October 2002, and convened by President Chirac and Prime Minister Hariri to help find ways of helping the Lebanese economy focused specifically on extending the maturity of the national

6

debt - $30 billion (around 200% of GDP) which had accumulated as the country recovered during the 1990s from 15 years of war and to reduce its servicing cost. As a direct result of implementation of the government's programme for further fiscal and structural reforms and privatisation of state owned utilities the budget deficit should start shrinking and, if current goals are achieved the budget is should balance by 2005. The national debt can then start declining.

The Bekaa valley

The traveller between Damascus and Beirut must cross the Bekaa Valley. This beautiful and fertile valley high in the Lebanese Mountains has many little treasures; the temple of Baalbak, the restaurants of Zahlé, and the wine caves of Ksara and the village of Chtaura. This latter village is the most improbable place for a banking and shopping centre, but such is the case. During the civil war and even after, citizens of Syria and expatriate workers would cross from Damascus to shop and deposit their money in one of the many banks. Because normal banking facilities did not exist in Syria, the Lebanese established a friendly neighbourhood bank just over the border. Having made their transactions, the Syrians were then persuaded to spend their money on luxury food stuffs, unavailable in their own country, at the many supermarkets of the village.

Tourism

Lebanon is keen to re-develop its tourism industry and to revitalise its pre-war image as the playground of the Middle East. As one of the more western countries of the Middle East, Lebanon is one of the closest to Europe. It offers major sporting activities from snow skiing to water skiing and from pot-holing to gambling, together with excellent facilities for tourists. The archaeological sites of the country are also legendary.

Fewer than a million tourists visit Lebanon each year, of which a little under half are Arabs. The number of Arab visitors has increased since September 11 2002 as they feel less welcome in the US. However, the average tourist spends about $2,000 during his stay. These figures encourage investors to develop tourist attractions and facilities. Despite the large number of hotels in existence, there is a continued enthusiasm for Lebanon from the big international groups; for example, Four Seasons, Intercontinental, Marriott, etc. Some of the former landmark hotels have been refurbished; the Phoenicia Intercontinental (probably the best at the moment), the Vendôme (with its famous Jimmy's Bar) and the newshound's favourite during the war, the Meridien Commodore. Sadly, the St Georges Hotel, much loved by the intelligence fraternity, has yet to be rejuvenated.

Lebanon is a small country but it is packed with things to do both day and night. There are many historical sites to visit, many forms of entertainment – nightclubs, restaurants and bars – many ways for the energetic to indulge their sporting desires, and all of it easily accessible.

Lebanese Wine

Lebanon has been famous for its wines for centuries. Although small in comparison to France and the New World wine regions, its production is excellent. Most Lebanese will enthuse about their wines and everyone will have their favourite and be able to quote good and bad years. A visit to the larger local supermarkets will demonstrate exactly the care and attention the Lebanese give their wines. Different Chateaux will have their wines laid out by the year, with prices reflecting the quality of a particular vintage.

To sit by the Mediterranean Sea in the sunshine or to dine outside amongst the pine-forested mountains at night, sipping the local wines, has to be one of Lebanon's most pleasurable experiences. Add to this the wonderful fresh fruit and vegetables that will adorn any good repast, then you have a truly memorable occasion.

6

Wine

Agriculture

Agriculture accounts for about 15 per cent of Lebanon's GDP and employs almost half the workforce. Despite these impressive figures there is a general malaise in this industry. Traditional farming methods, limited export markets, damaged infrastructure and degraded land as a result of the civil war all contribute to this decline in agro industry.

Lebanon has excellent natural resources for agriculture – fertile land, plentiful rain, abundant sunshine and proximity to the European and Middle Eastern markets. **Fruit** and **vegetables**, **olives** and **tobacco** are the principal crops grown in the country. The ancient tobacco-growing industry supports an equally archaic cigarette production industry. Fruit and vegetables are grown throughout the country.

Wine however, is the single success story in this otherwise depressed industry. Several excellent varieties of wine are made and are exported to Europe. Musar, Ksara and Kefraya wines are the most common and are available in UK outlets.

Education

The Lebanese literacy rate is about 90 per cent – one of the highest in the Arab world (Egypt's rate, for example, is about half this). About half the country's schools are private or State-aided and offer a final Lebanese Baccalaureate certificate based upon the European system. Some schools still offer an English language curriculum, with the Broummana High School being the most prestigious.

Lebanon has many good universities. The major Arabic language public university is the University of Lebanon, which has a new campus. The American University of Beirut (AUB) is the most famous and most prestigious of all education establishments in Lebanon and probably the Middle East. Others such as St Joseph University (Jesuit) Lebanese American University and Balamand University are well regarded.

Communications

In the 1960s and 1970s Lebanon thrived on international trade. Foreign companies set up their regional headquarters in Lebanon because of the communications – transport links and telecommunications.

In the early 1990s the prewar telecommunications system, barely operational, was the first part of the infrastructure to be modernised. Inevitably the Lebanese went for the latest and the best and installed one of the most up-to-date *systems* telecommunications in the world. Lebanon's information and communications industry was established and has become one of the

6

Telecommunications

government's largest sources of revenue. If, as is likely, this industry is privatised, it could once again take the lead as Lebanon's major source of income.

Early Printing Press

In the north of Lebanon, amongst the foothills of the Lebanese mountains, there are several communities established by holy men. One of these is famous for introducing printing to the Middle East in the 16th century. Visitors to this active monastery of Saint Anthony can see one of the original printing presses, which was imported from Scotland.

The logistics of getting such a large piece of machinery to such a remote location perched on the side of a mountain must have given the engineers more than a headache. Many of those involved in this exercise never made it home! In a cave adjacent to the monastery can be seen the chains fixed to the rock where the insane were chained in the hope that St Anthony would cure them. History does not recall how many Scots suffered this fate!

Printing

6

Media

The Lebanese media and entertainment sectors always flourished. Despite the war, or even because of it, huge numbers of small radio and television stations operated – over 100 radio and about 80 TV stations. Any self respecting militia group would expect to have one or both. In the mid 1990s the government brought in legislation to curb these excesses, so that today the numbers have fallen dramatically with 8 TV stations and about 50 radio stations. Television is supplied terrestrially or by satellite and cable.

In print, too, Lebanon is a country of plenty, with 13 daily newspapers and hundreds of magazines covering every possible aspect of life in and out of Lebanon. There is one English-language daily and one long-established French newspaper. For many years Lebanon has been an important centre for printing which has enabled it to maintain a high standard of modern technology. Many magazines from around the world, even some from Britain, are printed there.

Lebanon is also a regional leader in advertising. Advertising on the streets in newspapers, magazines and on television is very sophisticated and well presented.

Beirut Central District

The BCD is an ambitious and so far successful plan to rebuild the centre of Beirut. Old buildings have been renovated and unsightly ones demolished. Some areas are given over to pedestrians and to street cafés and restaurants. An old cinema has been tastefully converted into a Virgin Megastore. Areas of archaeological interest have been exposed for public viewing and other artefacts, especially mosaics, have been removed to the National Museum. The area which includes churches, mosques and the Parliament buildings will soon boast the planned Garden of Forgiveness which will link the three cathedrals and three mosques. Hotels have reopened and others are being built. Office shop space is now at a premium and prices for property to buy or rent have increased dramatically.

Adjacent to the BCD and the Port is the **Normandy Landfill**. During the war this was where the people of West Beirut tipped their rubbish – into the sea. In the early 1990s this landfill area was literally a mountain of evil-smelling rubbish and rubble. In order to reclaim the valuable land and use it for building, with all the attendant ecological and environmental difficulties, it was decided to remove and recycle its contents. Every bucketful of rubbish down to the original sea bed has been excavated and sorted into its many components – tyres, concrete, household and medical waste, munitions, earth, human remains, etc. It started as a major environmental project, but has now delivered to the BCD many hectares of additional land for development.

6

Normandy Landfill

Environmental and Construction Industries

After the war the programme to rebuild Lebanon was a priority. Inevitably, at the forefront of this drive was the reconstruction of the infrastructure. Organisations such as Solidére, the Council for Development and Reconstruction (CDR) and others were set up to monitor and oversee the work. Such organisations, while considered a private enterprise, were very much involved with public and private funds. To carry out the work many local and international contractors developed their capabilities and presence in Lebanon. To supply these industries construction material plants were established or existing ones regenerated.

Cement plants were the major sector to be revitalised, with foreign manufacturers looking to renew their associations with local companies. These companies became the driving force on the local stock market. The cement industry today is not efficiently run and has export capabilities, partly brought about as local construction slows down.

Other material manufacturers also developed their output to cope with the expected building boom. **Ceramics, aluminium, plastics, pipes,** were some of the major industries concerned.

Some of the major projects undertaken in the last decade have been the Beirut Central District (BCD) which is ongoing, a new airport with a runway for international flights, major highways (including a ring road and highway to Damascus), marine ports (including the Normandy Landfill) and housing and property development.

Other industries

There are of course many smaller sectors of industry in Lebanon though there is no heavy industry. **Textiles** and **leather,** which under intense competition from other regions has declined, could, under the new partnership with Europe, recover. **Pharmaceuticals** are a growing and specialised market exporting to Arab and Western countries. **Jewellery** manufacture, very close to many Lebanese women's hearts, is carried out mainly by the Armenian community in small workshops. The quality

6

(and the price) is high and it is therefore aimed at a specialist market. (see chapter 10, p133)

Another industry which sprung up after the war is the international **exhibition** industry. This somewhat unusual source of revenue started as a result of the enthusiasm and need for the reconstruction of the country and its industry. From relatively small beginnings in large tents, this has now grown to several permanent exhibition sites around the country, with displays of food, office equipment, antiques, machinery, fashion, telecoms, building materials, etc. There are also plans to develop a major conference centre overlooking the Mediterranean Sea near the Beirut Central District.

6

7

setting up a
permanent operation

setting up a
permanent operation

The aim of this section is to
provide a sweeping overview for
the visitor who is considering the
possibility of a local office. Here
are some of the pitfalls and
benefits, an insight into the legal
situation, and some of the major
issues to be considered, such as
recruiting, finding premises, etc.

Establishing a Presence

Lebanon has a very Western approach to business and is keen to encourage foreign investment and involvement in trade. While the Prime Minister is currently a businessman it can be expected that the laws of the country will encourage such trade. Indeed, if Lebanon is to become a member of the WTO several issues relating to taxation and intellectual copyright have to be, and are being, addressed.

When arriving in Lebanon a foreign company should try to retain its independence. It should avoid becoming dependent upon well-meaning 'agents' or partners unless otherwise advised by reliable local institutions. There are well-known instances of joint ventures in Lebanon where expatriate staff have been totally reliant upon a local organisation for support. However financially attractive it might seem to be whilst negotiating a deal, resist the temptation of any offers of support that are not strictly necessary. Allow foreign staff to choose their own accommodation and also allow them to make their own transport arrangements and buy cars and appoint drivers. The alternative to this engenders distrust and a feeling by the resident expatriate that his local colleagues are not allowing him full independence. All-inclusive rates for foreign staff should make administration much more straightforward and it avoids any misunderstandings.

Expatriate staff will soon become acquainted with the social scene in the country. Those with sporting interests and with children at one of the many schools will soon meet many others. Because most expatriates remain in one country for a relatively short time, everyone makes a greater effort to socialise. Business groups also offer the executive the opportunity to discuss problems that might arise.

Lebanon is a country where privatisation seems the obvious system, and where many experienced bankers and financiers are on hand to guide the process through. Indeed Lebanon has one of the first privatised postal systems in the world.

Lebanon and its government are also at the forefront of the international community in encouraging its institutions to embrace modern technology – for

7

example, bank branches have to be connected electronically on line.

Operating in Lebanon

A foreign company may establish a joint stock company, a limited liability company or a branch office. Both joint stock and limited liability companies require an appointed board with a Lebanese majority and a minimum capital (currently) of LL30m and LL5m respectively. Limited liability companies are restricted in their types of business and activity.

Any foreign company may open a branch office in Lebanon to undertake any business activity that falls under that company's Articles of Association. Regulations and registration are generally simple. There are no minimum capital requirements, but, as in most countries, the office must be registered with the Ministry of Economy and a *commercial court*. The manager of the office can be a foreigner provided he has a residence and work permit.

A foreign company may also open a representative office, but in this case they may not become involved with any commercial activity in Lebanon.

There are also: **Partnerships,** where foreign and local partners enter into business.

Joint Ventures, where foreign and local companies combine to undertake a specific project, usually a construction project.

Holding companies generally related to stock holdings and **offshore companies** relating to work outside Lebanon.

Foreign Investment

Of course, Lebanon is actively seeking foreign investment. Lebanon's legislative framework makes the country one of the most open economies and one of the most attractive places to invest in the region. In order to encourage this investment the government has set up the Investment Development Authority of Lebanon (IDAL) to provide services to investors, such as information on permits and licenses, coordination of private and public

7

IDAL

services, information on setting up companies, etc. IDAL can be found at [www.idal.com.lb].

Laws affecting Companies operating in Lebanon

Taxation Laws

The taxation system in Lebanon offers many attractions to a foreign investor. The principal regulations are to be found in Decree 144 of 1959, which has been amended by Decree 27/80 in 1980 and 282 in 1993. Laws 45 and 46 of 1993 refer to the position on offshore and holding companies. Lebanon considers profit or income generated in Lebanon liable for taxation, whether personal or corporate.

Personal taxation is imposed on all income, including salary, bonuses, allowances, etc, whether or not the individual is resident in Lebanon. The current rate (2002) starts at 2 per cent and increases to a maximum of 20 per cent. There are also exemptions for certain classes of employment – such as – clergy, nurses, the disabled – and allowances made for certain expenses, for example, pensions, children, etc. The income tax, deducted at source by the employer, is paid every six months.

Corporate tax, as with personal tax, is based upon any income relating to business with Lebanon. There is a general flat rate tax of 15 per cent plus a 10 per cent tax on distribution of dividends. Here, too, there are the inevitable exceptions and exemptions; indefinite for certain business groups (educational, hospitals, farmers, etc.), and a ten-year exemption for companies active in certain development zones or producing new products. Companies re-investing in their business also receive tax breaks. There are also deductible expenses, depreciation and, of course, losses, which are included in any taxation calculation.

Non-resident companies are subject to special treatment and a withholding tax is usually applied on exported profits – a local auditor will advise more detail (a great many of the international names in auditing have a presence). Such taxes are withheld by the Lebanese customer and passed on to the authorities. Public works

Income Tax

7

Corporate Tax

contractors are also deemed to make a profit on the value of their contract and are taxed accordingly.

Social Security

There is also a Social Security system with income derived from both employees and employers. Employers pay 12 per cent to the sickness programme, 15 per cent to the family allowance programme and 8.5 per cent to the end-of-service fund. Employees pay a flat 3 per cent to the sickness fund.

Expatriates are also subjected to these rates unless they can show that they are contributing to a similar scheme in their home country.

Other taxes which affect the individual or company include capital gains, estate and gift tax and stamp duties.

VAT

A law was passed in February 2002 establishing a Value Added Tax of 10 per cent on most goods and services, except for basic foodstuffs, such as bread and vegetables.

Lebanon does not yet have a double taxation agreement with the UK or US. Such agreements exist for some European and regional countries.

7

Practicalities of Opening an Office

The location of an office is clearly very important. Criteria such as access to the airport and ring-road are significant. Is it possible for customers and clients to visit and park their cars near the office? This is important, although most Lebanese will have a driver who will be adept at dropping their passengers off and being outside at the right time for collection. Some areas are more suited to business operations. Some areas are served better by terrestrial telephone lines. Television or radio signals are obscured in some locations. Should the office be near the home and, if so, should home be near a school?

Office Location

The main area for offices in Beirut has recently become the Beirut Central District (BCD). Property, when available, commands significant rates both for sale (rare) and for rent. The Hamra area remains traditionally popular.

Communications

Communications for businesses are reliable as a result of the introduction of mobile phones in the 1990s and the excellent new telecommunication infrastructure. The use of internet and electronic mail, introduced at the same time, has become an everyday tool for the modern business executive and perhaps more easily accessible than in Europe or America.

Domestic couriers are used extensively throughout Lebanon to deliver mail and messages. International courier services are also widely available.

Staff

Before the war, Lebanon claimed to have the best-trained workforce in the region. This well-trained pool of staff enabled the country to maintain its reputation for service and skills. After twenty years of war these high standards have slipped. The government is aware of this and is trying to introduce vocational training schemes for young people. However, at the senior level, the country can boast some of the best professionals in the region; engineers, lawyers, doctors and, of course, bankers.

7

Labour and staff wages in Lebanon are low by European and American standards, but high in relation to neighbouring countries. The following is a guide to the level of monthly salaries that might be expected in 2002:

Driver	$200 - $600
Secretary	$500 - $1000
Office Manager	$1000 - $2000
Senior Manager	$3000 - $6000
Accountant	$800 - $1500
Senior Accountant	$1500 - $3000

Many Lebanese attend university and are highly qualified, but like elsewhere in the world it has become more difficult for graduates to find employment.

Working Hours

The Lebanese – starting at 0800 and finishing late in the evening. Government offices follow sensible rules, unlike most of their neighbours in the Middle East. The weekend (unlike most Islamic countries) falls on Saturday and Sunday. Most shops are closed on Sunday, although the advent of large supermarkets has introduced 24-hour shopping.

Transport

There are limited bus services and taxis, but otherwise the employees and employers of Lebanon have a common form of transport – the motor car. This leads to serious rush-hour traffic jams. Although the roads between the cities, and to some extent within Beirut, are wide and free-flowing, the narrow side streets, congested with parked cars, are a nightmare – combine this with Beirut's hilly topography and you have chaos!

Areas like the Beirut Central District (BCD) have car parks. This, together with the arterial roads that link it, make the BCD decidedly attractive. Many apartment blocks/offices have underground parking, possibly with memories of the war – most buildings, even today, have large basements which can be used as a refuge in times of conflict. Since most Lebanese own at least one car, parking is a problem.

It is not uncommon for office staff to spend long hours travelling from home to the office. Journeys of over an hour are usual, with the poorer staff living in the more remote areas, which are inevitably less well provided with public transport.

7

8

Beirut

Beirut

Beirut is the capital of Lebanon, described in former times as the Riviera of the Middle East. The city is situated on a promontory in the Mediterranean Sea facing north and west. This location leads to the geographical divisions of East and West Beirut and causes the newcomer to the city confusion when trying to orientate himself with the coastline!

History of Beirut

It is suggested that the city is named after a well or wells of Birut. Indeed the modern Arabic for well is *bir*. The Roman Emperor Augustus named the city in honour of his daughter Julia, so that the full title became Colonia Julia Augusta Felix Berytus.

Traces of Stone Age settlements have been found in the city at the mouth of the Beirut River. Canaanite remains, dating back about 4000 years, have been found in recent excavations, together with remains of the Phoenician civilisation.

8

The Past Unearthed

During the civil war, the downtown area of Beirut, now becoming the Beirut Central District, became a no-go area. It was also at one end of the Green Line, where opposing militias faced each other for many years. The destruction of the city and the post-war government's policy to rebuild the area completely, presented archaeologists with a unique opportunity to excavate the old city area. The true extent of the ancient city was revealed. In addition, further, deeper excavations revealed remains of older civilisations.

Although most of these excavations will be covered up, there remain areas amongst the new and refurbished buildings where visitors can get a flavour of the ancient city.

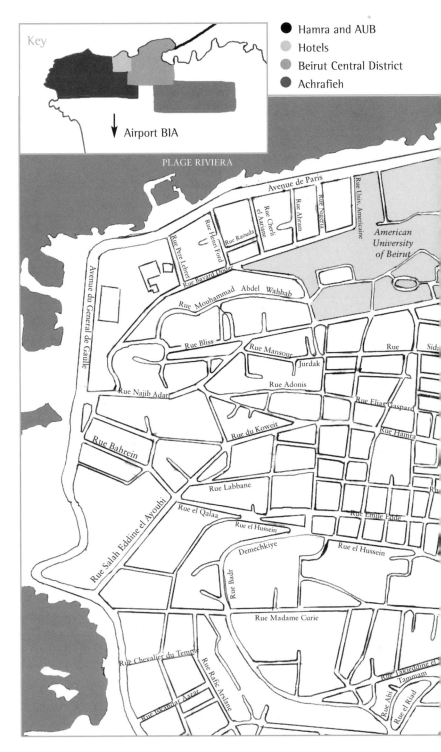

Beirut Hamra and American University

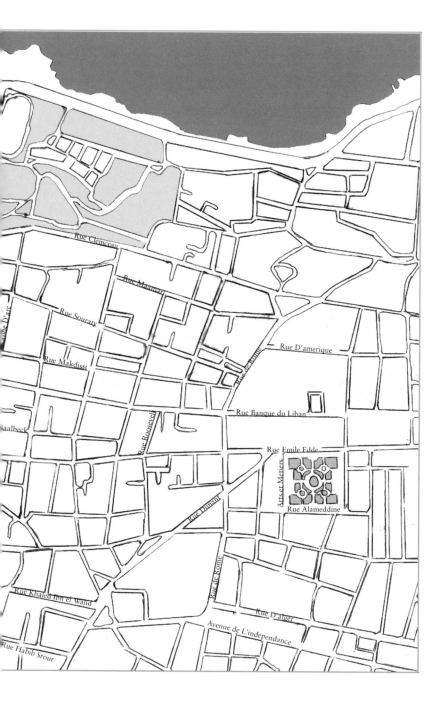

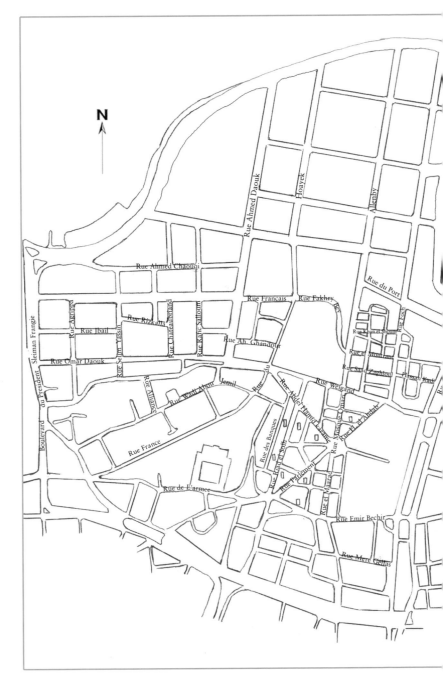

Beirut Central District

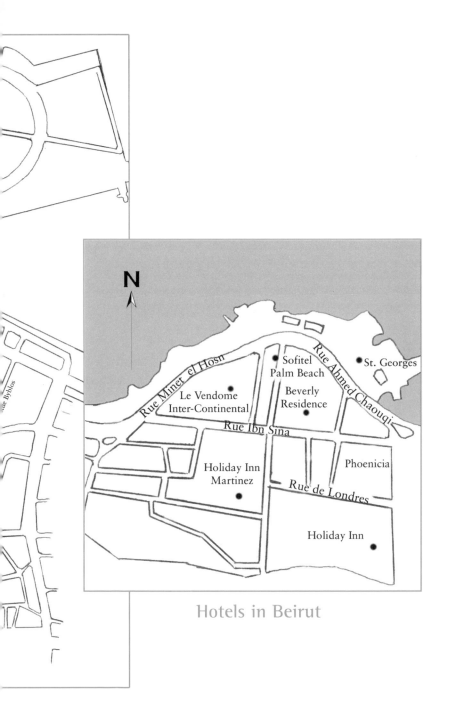

Hotels in Beirut

Beirut Achrafieh

ACHRAFIEH

The first historical reference to Beirut was found in Egypt. Stone tablets from the 14th century BC record that the Canaanite King of Beirut asked for military assistance from the Egyptian Pharaoh. In Phoenician times other Lebanese towns, for example, Sidon and Tyre, overshadowed the city. Extensive references exist dating from Greek times and from the period of Alexander the Great, who laid the foundation for the Roman city.

The Romans built a major city on the site, some remains of which can be seen today. Public buildings, baths and temple ruins are visible throughout the city and artefacts are on view in the museum. The famous School of Law was established in the 3rd century AD and the basis of the Justinian Code, from which Western codes of law have been derived, was conceived here.

In the 5th century AD severe earthquakes and tidal waves almost destroyed the city, so that when the Arab conquerors arrived in the 7th century they met little resistance. The city passed from Arab to Crusader hands and back again on several occasions over the next centuries, until finally control passed to the Mamelukes at the end of the 13th Century.

The city was again conquered in the 16th century by the Ottomans and became an autonomous city-state. During this period, Beirut began to develop trade with Europe, and Venice in particular. A brief romance with Mohamed Ali in Egypt followed until the Europeans, in particular the British, Austrians and Turks, restored the city to the Ottoman Empire. By the end of the First World War the Ottoman Empire had crumbled and the British and French occupied the city until, in 1920, the League of Nations granted a French mandate over Syria and Lebanon, and Beirut became the capital of Greater Lebanon.

How to Get about

Cars are probably the most likely form of transport for a foreign business traveller. There are a few cyclists and also the inevitable motor scooters and motor bikes. These two-wheeled forms of transport are probably the most convenient and most dangerous and are much used by couriers and suicidal pizza delivery boys!

8

Where to live

Areas like Achrafieh within the city and the Beirut
Central District are the favoured places to live. Those
with a generous budget might also choose to live
overlooking the sea. Hamra is the old centre of Beirut,
with Rue Hamra being the shopping centre. Many
foreigners live in this area as it is convenient for most
offices, Ministries, etc; but it is the most congested area
of the city. Ras Beirut, another favoured area, is also
near the Rue Verdun, which claims to have some of the
most expensive shops in the world!

Those with offices to the north of the city may choose
Jounieh, a suburb which grew up after the war. This
small town is well equipped with facilities such as
restaurants, hotels, shops, etc, but is a little far away
from the airport which is to the south of the city.

Those wanting peace and quiet and not concerned about
a long drive to the office may choose the cooler climes of
the hills and mountains to the east of the city. Towns like
Broummana and Beit Meri offer good alternatives.
Broummana has a very good British-orientated school –
the Broummana High School, where leading Anglophiles
from around the Middle East went to school. The
disadvantage of being in the hills – its distance from
central Beirut and the winter cold – are probably out-
weighed by the clean mountain air and spectacular views
for most of the year.

8

The Corniche

The Lebanese are preoccupied with their appearance.
Exercise is all-important and equally vital to be seen to
be exercising and to be smartly dressed for the
occasion. Early every morning on the Corniche in front
of the American University from Ras Beirut to the BCD,
the smart folk of Beirut can be seen in their designer
exercise wear, jogging, running or gently walking up
and down, ritually acknowledging their fellows.

If you think that it is only possible to look good when
dressed for a cocktail party, then get up early one
morning and take the sea air on the Corniche.

Hotels

Beirut, and Lebanon in general, has no shortage of good hostelries for all budgets, from cheap backpacking hostels to five-star luxury hotels. Service everywhere is impeccable and hotels and restaurants are clean and hygenic. Those travellers who remember the Beirut of pre-war days will doubtless remember the Phoenicia and the St George's Hotels. The former has been returned to its earlier glory, if without its 1960s exclusivity, but sadly the St George's, with its romantic cloak-and-dagger connections, remains a shell. Those hardy expatriates will recall the Mayflower Hotel with the Duke of Wellington Bar (just opposite the Napoleon Hotel) as the venue for pre-party drinks on a Friday night. Those who braved the country during the war will recall the Commodore Hotel and its famous parrot that livened up the bar where all the newshounds compared notes. The foremost hotel during and after the war was Le Bristol, with bullet holes in the glass, and the two levels of basements where guests were assured of security and comfort throughout the war.

Hotels in Lebanon can easily be found on the internet at either [www.lebanon.com] or at [www.1stlebanon.net] or from their own websites. They can be expensive (some very expensive), but they will offer good service and comfort. Hotels are generally small with up to 200 rooms and thus are intimate and friendly. They tend not to have big atriums and public areas. Always ask for a room with a view.

The Phoenicia Intercontinental

This is probably the most prestigious of all the hotels in the country. Overlooking St Georges Bay and adjacent to the BCD the hotel offers excellent facilities for guests and visitors. A favourite venue for the glitterati to show off at receptions and functions. A swimming pool and the usual health facilities for tired executives are available.

❏ Tel: (01) 369 100; fax: (01) 369 101
Website: [www.intercontinental.com]
[http//beirut-phoenicia.lebanon.intercontinental.com]
E-mail: [Phoenicia@interconti.com]

Le Vendôme Intercontinental

A smaller hotel, adjacent to its big cousin Phoenicia, also on the waterfront. Very popular for its roof-top bar named after one of its famous barmen – Sydney. Comfortable and convenient location with reasonable road access to the rest of the city and the airport. It is also close to the Hard Rock Café and other night clubs for those trendy night-owls.

❑ Tel: (01) 369 280; fax: (01) 369 169
Web pages: [www.intercontinental.com]
[http//Beirut-levendome.Lebanon.intercontinental.com]
E-mail: [Beirut@interconti.com]

The Riviera Hotel
A relatively small and friendly private hotel, located on the edge of the Corniche, it has great views of the sea (and the beautiful people exercising in the morning). Comfortable rooms and modest dining facilities. One of the first five-star hotels to be renovated after the war. Its main attraction is the wonderful swimming pool and marina, which is accessible via a tunnel under the main road. These facilities are also available to locals on a club membership basis – definitely the place to be seen.

❑ Tel: (01) 373 210 – 9; fax: (01) 365 239
Website: www.rivierahotel.com.lb
E-mail: [info@rivierahotel.com.lb]

Le Bristol
This hotel retains its French connection. Situated inland on the hill above the shopping centre of Hamra and equidistant from the west and north coast of Beirut, it is one of the grand old private hotels and still much used by the Lebanese for functions. The whole hotel has been renovated since the war and offers good accommodation. Its basement, which once housed an ice rink and dining and reception facilities, is now used for conferences and exhibitions.

❑ Tel: (01) 351 400; fax: (01) 351 409
Website: [www.lebristol-hotel.com]
E-mail: [Bristol@dm.net.lb]

Le Meridien Commodore
Just off Rue Hamra, its location is ideal for those who like to roam the streets of Beirut looking at the shops. Good hotel catering for business clients. Ask about the parrot in the bar!

❑ Tel: (01) 350 400; fax: (01) 345 806
Website: [www.lemeridien.com]
E-mail: [sales@lemeridien-commodore.com]

8

Holiday Inn Martinez
Convenient well-equipped hotel near the BCD and sea front. Also very near various night time entertainments.

❑ Tel: (01) 368 111; fax: (01) 370 333
Website: [www.sixcontinenthotels.com/holiday-inn]
E-mail: [sales@holidayinn-martinez.com]

Holiday Inn Dunes
Situated in the expensive area of Verdun.

❑ Tel: (01) 792 111; fax: (01) 792 333
Website: [www.holidayinn-dunes.com]

Summerland Hotel
One of the few hotels actually on the sea side of the road near the airport. It was built during the war and provided the élite of the city with some comfort during those difficult times. It also boasted its own militia to protect that élite. Still popular with the Gulf Arabs. Also near the golf course.

❑ Tel: (01) 858 000; fax: (01 856 666
Website: [www.summerland.com.lb]
E-mail: [info@summerland.com.lb]

Marriott Hotel
The Marriott was built just after the war and was one of the first major chain hotels to reopen in the city. Convenient for the airport and the golf course.

❑ Tel: (01) 840 540; fax: (01) 840 345
Website: [www.marriotthotels.com]

Mayflower Hotel
The Mayflower and the Duke of Wellington bar are part of Lebanese expatriate life. Very popular and centrally located in Hamra, it is an ideal place to stay on a tight budget on a long-term basis – and there will always be some kindred spirit in the bar at the end of the day. Surrounded by good cheap cafés and restaurants.

❑ Tel: (01) 340 680; fax: (01)342 038
Website: [www.mayflower.com.lb]
E-mail: [mayflo@dm.net.lb]

Marble Tower Hotel
Another budget hotel in central Hamra. Good, clean and accessible.

❑ Tel: (01) 354 586; fax: (01) 346 262

Mercure Berkeley Hotel
Good, clean and cheap in Hamra. This chain offers
reasonable accommodation.

❑ Tel: (01) 340 600; fax: 602 250

For a really unique and extravagant Lebanese experience
there are two other privately-owned and expensive hotels
that should not be missed. Even if you cannot afford to
stay, a visit to their restaurants is an unforgettable
experience.

The Albergo Hotel
This hotel is in the centre of Beirut in a converted house
on one of the typical side streets. It is most famous for its
Italian restaurant, al Dente. It has only 33 rooms/suites,
which can be seen and booked on its rather innovative
website. Well worth a visit.

❑ Tel: (01) 339 797; fax (01) 339 999
Website: [www.albergobeirut.com]
E-mail: [albergo@relaischateaux.fr]

Al Bustan Hotel
Although not very convenient for Beirut, this wonderful
hotel in the mountains, with magnificent views of the sea
and set amongst the pine forests, is a refuge from the
hustle and bustle of Beirut life. It has wonderful food and
restaurants and is worth a visit even if a stay is
impossible. A summer arts and music festival makes this
hotel very well known by the international élite.

❑ Tel: (04) 870 400; fax (04) 972 439
E-mail: [hotel@albustan.lb.com]
Website: [www.albustanhotel.com]

Two well known names in the hotel industry arrived in
Beirut in 2002 – a Mövenpick and a Crown Plaza.

The Mövenpick Hotel is situated in the Raouche area
and has its own beach.

❑ Tel: (01) 869 666; fax: (01) 809 326
E-mail: [resort.Beirut@movenpick.com]
Website: [www.movenpick-beirut.com]

The Crown Plaza is in central Beirut in the Hamra
district, in Hamra Street itself.

❑ Tel: (01) 754 755; fax (01) 749 555
Website: [www.cpbeirut.com]

8

Restaurants in and around Beirut

Sadly there are not enough days in the week or mealtimes in a day to experience the wonders of the Lebanese restaurants. Apart from the Lebanese meals, which tend to be gargantuan and never ending, international cuisine is also served with similar perfection. For a snack or something to nibble between meals, don't be afraid to stop at any street corner for a *shwerma* or a sandwich.

Sitting overlooking the sea and sampling the food and local wines, or drinking local *arak* is an experience not to be missed – use a fresh glass for the arak so that it goes a milky colour after adding water or ice, and not before. Sit under the pine trees in the hills overlooking the Mediterranean Sea at night and sample the *mezze,* fresh fruit and vegetables, locally caught fish (especially the 'sultan brahim', the deep fried red mullet). When you are feeling rather overfed and your host insists that you have a dessert, ask for the *ishtar*, a very light digestible dish of thick cream and honey.

Hotel restaurants are, as you might expect, graded to the standard of the hotel. However, with a few exceptions, they are hotel food outlets. Perhaps for this reason the most memorable food experiences are not to be had in hotel eateries. The places below are just a small list of places which achieve culinary heights.

For a complete list of Lebanese restaurants and other places to go at night go to [www.lebanonnights.com].

Al Dente - Italian
Situated in an old house (along with the Albergo Hotel) in central Beirut this legendary restaurant offers without doubt the very best of true Italian food. Set meals might prove a problem for those with small appetites, but it does avoid the usual lengthy deliberations.

❑ Tel: (01) 202 440

La Piazza – Italian
A very different approach to Italian food. A big open alfresco eatery in Sodeco district, with lots of atmosphere and bustling activity. Large pizza ovens. The sort of smart fun restaurant where you eat and drink lots.

❑ Tel: (01) 339 449

8

Scoozi – Italian

Situated on the edge of the Verdun district, this very trendy pizza house was one of the first fast-food restaurants to open after the war. Very popular with society nibblers and good for a quick snack.

❑ Tel: (01) 865489

Sushi – Japanese

One of many restaurants in Achrafieh. For those who like raw oriental food – you won't find better.

❑ Tel: (01) 337 888

China Moon – Asian

This Achrafieh restaurant has been a firm favourite with the local community for many years, as you can tell from the phone number.

❑ Tel: (01) 202 202

Jardin de Chine – Chinese

Unusual experience in that the food just comes – whatever is being cooked. Sumptuous surroundings, nice ambience and great food, of course in Jal el Dib.

❑ Tel: (04) 714665

8

L'Entrecote – French steak house

Another Achrafieh dive, where the surprising thing is that you can really only get steak and fries which come in two waves – you sit down, you order, you get served, you eat and then the waiter comes with more of the same! A shock for those that might have thought they were getting away with a light meal! Good fun.

❑ Tel: (01) 334 048

Le Rabelais – French

This is really one of the best places for French cuisine. Quiet, formal atmosphere and plenty of room, located in Achrafieh.

❑ Tel: (01 330 648

Al Mijana – Lebanese

Again in Achrafieh, this is probably the best and most formal of Lebanese restaurants in Beirut. Set in an old villa with a small outside eating area, this has to be the place to experience Lebanese food.

❑ Tel: (01) 328 082

La Petite Maree – Seafood

Probably the best seafood restaurant in central Beirut. In Achrafieh, this is the place where you choose your fish prior to cooking. Generally local fish, but also imported lobster and shell fish.

❏ Tel: (01) 204 111

These are a few of the restaurants of central Beirut. However, not far away are some alternatives for special occasions.

Jounieh

Jounieh has many good restaurants, about half-an-hour's drive to the north of Beirut. One restaurant in particular is a seaside, beach-fronted old house called **Chez Sami** (❏ tel: (09) 910520). This is another excellent fish restaurant. Bags of atmosphere and, with the sea almost lapping at your ankles, a wonderful place to spend a warm summer's evening.

Byblos

For a very memorable lunch the internationally famous **Byblos Fishing Club** (sometimes known as Chez Pépé) is a must. This fish restaurant overlooking the Roman Harbour and castle ruins of **Byblos** is about one-hour's drive north of Beirut. Watch the fish arrive, from the sea and not from a truck. Drink the chilled local white wine and you will understand why such celebrities as Bridget Bardot, Marlon Brando and David Niven were regular visitors (and see some unpublished pictures of BB with Pépé on the wall). ❏ Tel: (09) 540 213

Beit Meri

Broummana

For one of those gargantuan Lebanese feasts, head for the mountains (with a driver) and try **Mounir's**.
❏ Tel: (04) 873 900. Set amongst the pine trees of Beit Meri with an amazing view of the city and the sea beyond. Or the famous **Kasr Fakhredine** ❏ Tel: (01) 04 960407 where good Lebanese food is also available at this Broummana restaurant.

For a weekend buffet and relaxation head for the **Al Bustan Hotel** and sample the best of self-service menus, take it to the terrace and wallow in the enjoyment of food and the view of the Mediterranean Sea.

BCD

For those that like to wander around watching at others eat and like the street café atmosphere, head down to the **Beirut Central District** and take your pick – you won't be disappointed. Even Richard Branson's Virgin Megastore has a good eatery with a superb view of the old (new) city.

Recreation for the resident expatriate.

There is no shortage of things to do for the tired expat!
Health clubs and sport are important ways to pass the
weekend. Summer and winter there are different
pastimes to enjoy.

- Swimming

- Diving

- Wind surfing

- Beaches

- Walking

- Golf

- Potholing

- Climbing

- Camping

- Horse riding

- Hash house harriers – social running

- Gambling

- Nightclubs

- Cinema and theatre

- Jazz

- Classical music festivals

- Archaeological excursions

- Skiing

- Horse racing

- Paragliding

8

other major cities

9

other major cities

Lebanon is a one of those places where most people talk only of the capital, Beirut. However, there are other fine towns, the principal one being Tripoli in the north. Other towns like Sidon and Tyre in the south also have their unique identity – the well-known Prime Minister Rafiq Hariri comes from Sidon. Other towns nearer Beirut have become merged with the capital – Jounieh, for example. Byblos, half way between Tripoli and Beirut, is another significant town, known more for its tourist attractions than any commercial activity. Zahlé and Chtoura in the Bekaa Valley do have some commerce, like wine caves, banking facilities and agriculture.

Tripoli

Tripoli is about one and a half hour's drive north of Beirut and is the other main city of Lebanon. In the past, a railway ran between Beirut and Tripoli, which gradually declined until only one train a week ran from the cement works at Cheka down to the capital. Nowadays road transport is the only link between the two cities.

Tripoli is very different from Beirut and the people there are fiercely independent. They have their own commercial organisations, industry, and tourist attractions, aspire to have their own airport and have the principal oil refinery for the country. The city is much more like other regional cities and has a more Islamic feel about it. Old *suqs*, mosques and the Citadel are reminders of the region's religious past. There is little to remind one of the hedonistic pleasure-loving people from Beirut.

Tripoli

9

Tripoli

Tripoli refinery was for many years at one end of the oil pipeline from Iraq. The British-owned Iraq Petroleum Company owned and managed the pipeline and two refineries – one in Tripoli and the other in Banias, further north in Syria. The offices of the Tripoli refinery, which now merely receives crude oil by sea and refines it for home consumption, shows the logic of the British presence. The British are remembered fondly by the current management, many of whom remember the 'good old days' before the civil war. Standards and procedural manuals from that time are still used. The administration compound, with its well-kept lawns and rose gardens outside the director's office, recall British colonial orderlines. Faded pictures and memorabilia still festoon the office.

9

Tripoli, like most other old towns in the region, has a history of occupation, by Romans, Crusaders and other invaders. These occupiers left their mark on the city and developed it into a trading centre. Tripoli has one of the country's major commercial sea ports, which came into its own during the civil war, since the fighting was less intense in this area.

The Citadel

The city itself is dominated by the Citadel, a Crusader castle built by and named after Raymond de Saint-Gilles of Toulouse in the 12th century. Surrounding the Citadel is the old *suq* or market area. The pro-Arab nationalist forces of Rachid Karami held out in this labyrinth of streets during a civil uprising in the late 1950s and his name is commemorated in street names throughout the city and at the fairground on the outskirts of the city.

Where to stay

There are two main places to stay in Tripoli: **Le Chateau Des Oliviers** (usually known as Villa Nadia after the owner Nadia) and a newly-opened **Quality Inn,** by the Rachid Karami fairground. The Quality Inn is probably the most suitable for business people.

Villa Nadia can be found in the hills a few kilometres south of Tripoli. Guests are well looked after and a relaxing stay is assured.

❑ Tel: (06) 432 513; fax (06) 411 190
Website: [www.villanadia.com]
E-mail: [info@villanadia.com]

Quality Inn is on the site of the fairground and ideal for exhibitors and visitors to the fair. Part of the American chain of hotels, it offers good basic business accommodation.

❑ Tel: (06) 211 255; fax (06) 211 277
Website: [www.qualityinn.com]
E-mail: [qualityinn1@inco.com.lb]

There are several other coastal resort hotels. Not all are open all year round and generally only cater for local holidaymakers. Adequate, but probably best avoided.

Restaurants

Not such a culinary paradise as Beirut, nevertheless Tripoli does have some good Lebanese restaurants. Some of the cafés around the Citadel are worth a visit. Try **Al Balad** in the Place d'Etoile. Tripoli is famous for its pastries. One shop in particular, **Rafaat Hallab et Fills,** is famous throughout the world and its delicacies can be seen on its own website: [www.hallab.com].

Sidon and Tyre (Saida and Sour)

Forty-five kilometres to the south of Beirut lies the prosperous city of Sidon, and 40 kilometres further south lies the less fortunate Tyre.

Although Sidon is thought to have been inhabited as early as 4000 BC, both Sidon and Tyre reached a peak of prosperity during Phoenician times. **Tyre** was probably the most economically powerful and successful of all the Phoenician city states, but thereafter its fortunes fluctuated, peaking during the Roman and Byzantine era, and declining after the fall of the Crusaders. This decline has continued, and its proximity to the Israeli border and the ravages of the civil war have left the town with a sad, subdued air.

Tyre

Sidon, by contrast, is a prosperous place, a prosperity which owes much to the influence of its most famous son, former Prime Minister Rafiq Hariri, who instigated the reconstruction of the city after the war.

The city is famous for its purple dye, made from crushed molluscs. This highly-prized dye came to be used to

Sidon

colour the silks worn by emperors and rulers throughout the world. Both cities were also famed for their cedar wood, which was widely traded and used to build the great ships of seafaring Phoenicians.

Sidon's main attractions are the Sea Castle, built by the Crusaders in the 13th century, and the Great Mosque which, like the Great Mosque in Tripoli, was built on the remains of a Crusader church. It was built as a church in the 13th century and converted into a mosque by the Mamelukes.

Sidon's only hotel worth the name is the **Hotel d' Orient** (Nazel ash Sharq) with only six rooms. It is a far cry from the business class hotels in Tyre the best of which are the expensive **Abu-Dib Hotel** and the more modestly priced four-star **Government Rest House**

❑ Tel: (07) 740677; fax: (07) 345163

Jounieh

Jounieh is situated north of Beirut (it can even be considered a suburb of the capital) and, until the war, was no more than a fishing village.

Jounieh

The shelling of Beirut drove many people north, and the pressures of war led to a haphazard development of the city. Since much of the city is new, there is little of historical interest, but at night, with lively clubs, cafés, discos, cinemas and restaurants the town comes to life.

During the war, ferries ran between Jounieh and Cyprus and, when Beirut airport closed, it became one of the few points of access to the country. The port still thrives.

The Zouk and Kaslik areas of Jounieh are equally lively, the latter being the home of the Casino de Liban, and both areas have trendy shops and restaurants.

Places to stay
Regency Palace Hotel
❑ Tel: (09) 854 000; fax (09) 854 854
Website: [www.regencypalace.com.lb]
E-mail: [info@regencypalace.com.lb]

Portemilio Hotel
❑ Tel: (09) 933 300; fax (09) 931 866
E-mail: [portemilio@lebanon.com]

9

Century Park Hotel
❑ Tel: (09) 219 000; fax (09) 213 050
Website: [www.centuryparkhotel.com.lb]
E-mail: [info@centuryparkhotel.com.lb]

Bekaa Valley

The Bekaa Valley lies between the Mt. Lebanon range and the Anti-Lebanon range on the Syrian border. It is a fertile strip, once known as the breadbasket of the Roman Empire, though in recent decades it has suffered as a result of deforestation and neglect, and lack of government subsidies to help farmers compete with cheaper Syrian produce. Nonetheless, the wines of the Bekaa Valley are world famous. The first vineyard was established in **Ksara**, and the winery on the outskirts of **Zahlé** is open to visitors daily from 9 am to 3 pm.

Zahlé

Zahlé is also famous for its restaurants on the banks of the Birdawni River.

There are several good hotels:

Grand Hotel Kadri Hotel
Situated in Zahlé, the centre of wine growing in the valley and where the famous Ksara wine caves are located. Zahlé is also famous for its restaurants situated on the banks of the Birdawni River, which falls steeply from the mountains around.

9

❑ Tel: (08) 813 920; fax (08) 803 314
Website: [www.kadrotel.com.lb]
E-mail: [info@kadrotel.com.lb]

Palmyra Hotel
This hotel is situated in the centre of the town of **Baalbek**. The Roman ruins at Baalbek are probably the greatest tourist attraction in Lebanon, and the town is famous for its music festivals. This music extravaganza has attracted the best musicians from around the world for many years, many of whom have left a record of their stay in the hotel. The hotel is over 120 years old and has been variously used by German and British occupying forces as their headquarters. It retains its Victorian charm. Definitely worth a visit, if not a stay.

Baalbek

❑ Tel: (08) 370 230/370 011; fax: (08) 370 305

Massabki Hotel - Chtaura
Recently refurbished, it is on the main road to Damascus, with good rooms and service.

❑ Tel: (03) 709 710

9

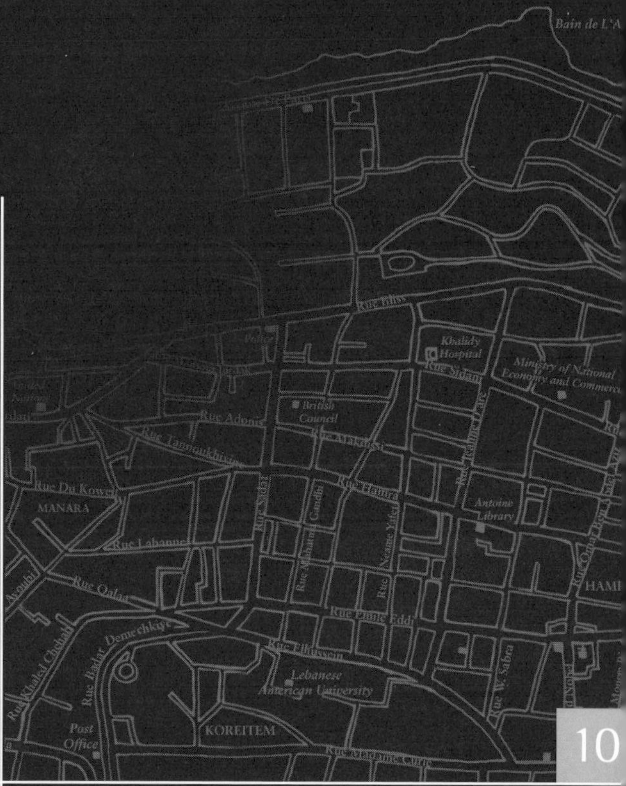

10

a break from business

a break from business

From what to do in a spare
afternoon to possible reasons for
delaying your flight back.

You may be busy doing business, but it is worth making time to take in some of the sites, ancient and modern, of this beautiful country.

The climate in Lebanon is generally very agreeable and ideal for sightseeing. Even in the summer, temperatures are rarely unbearable, although close to the sea it can be humid. However, relief is never far away with mountain retreats within a few minutes, drive.

Within the city of Beirut itself there are many archaeological sites, those in the **Beirut Central District** being the most noteworthy and accessible. If ruins don't interest you, take a look at the architecture itself, especially in the BCD, where many buildings have been restored to their former glory. Many have become cafés and offices. Even the Virgin Megastore, which was once a cinema, is worth a look. There are two mosques in **Martyr's Square** and two cathedrals worth visiting both called St Georges at Nijuieh Square close to Martyr's Square. Visit the **museum**, which was close to the Green Line and serious fighting; the artefacts were saved, the museum refurbished and the exhibits replaced. Wander around the old shopping area of **Hamra**, or if you are celebrating, visit the **Verdun** area and be wildly extravagant. Or get up early in the morning and saunter or jog along the **Corniche** by the American University of Beirut.

For those with a little more time and with a good excuse, head up to the mountains. Stop in Broummana or Beit Meri and look at the shops, the view and the cafés. Continue further into the mountains and visit the village of Aley on the road to Damascus. Whilst in the mountains stop for lunch or dinner (see chapter 8, p102).

Half-day excursions

Byblos

One of the most pleasant and relaxing tourist sites can be found at **Byblos**. However if such a visit is planned allow an extra half an hour to stop at the Dog River – on emerging from the tunnel on the coast road, park and climb up and over the exit. Monuments and graffiti can be found commemorating the various armies that have stopped here before heading over the bluff to Beirut. Monuments in Arabic, Greek, Latin, English and French – even a memorial to Nebuchadnesar – can be seen.

10

Byblos (or Jbail as it is known locally) is one of the oldest continually inhabited towns, dating back some 7000 years. In the 3rd millennium BC the Phoenicians established a city-state here, which developed close links with Egypt. The export of Cedar timber for the Pharaonic temples being one of the main items of trade and later the transhipment of papyrus from Egypt to Greece. The small Crusader castle and the temples and theatres surrounding dominate the seaside archaeological sites. From the castle a short walk takes the visitor to the Roman harbour and to the cafés and restaurants.

Chouf Mountains

These mountains lie to the south east of Beirut and are part of the Mount Lebanon range. **The Beit ed-dine Palace** is a significant monument in the mountains, which was built in the 18th/19th century by the then ruler of Mount Lebanon, Emir Shihab. The Palace is home to various museums, the most important being of Byzantine mosaics. There is also an arts festival held there every summer.

10

Tyre and Sidon

These two towns south of Beirut are worth an excursion – see chapter 9.

Jeita Grotto

To the north of Beirut these series of **caves and grottos** contain some of the best examples of stalactites and stalagmites in the world. The main cave stretches more than 5 kilometres into the hillside. Only discovered in the middle of the 19th century by a visitor on a hunting trip, these caves have become one of Lebanon's major tourist attractions. They were used as an ammunition store during the war and were reopened to the public in 1995.

Caves

Bsous Silk Museum

Situated about 20 minutes, drive from Beirut. Discover how silk was produced in Lebanon until the 1950s. Situated in a beautiful garden overlooking a green valley, the museum was built in the late 19th century and constitutes a leading example of the Lebanese architecture at the time. Open May/June and October/November or by appointment.

❏ Tel: (05) 940 767

Mummies

I had been a regular visitor to Lebanon for some time after the war and had got to know many Lebanese businessmen and officials. During one of my spells in the UK I was in a waiting room idly flicking through *Hello* magazine (as one does) when I came across an article on Lebanon. The story was that during the war potholers were exploring some of the caves in the Lebanese mountains when they came across some 13th century Christian mummified bodies in one of these caverns. The amateur enthusiasts had resisted doing much about the find, except to record the position, take photographs and to remove some artefacts as proof that some burial chamber existed. It was only after hostilities ceased that the full extent of the find was published and the mummies removed to the Beirut museum.

Hello magazine had chosen to cover this story – probably one of its more serious articles.

10

Day excursions

Baalbek

One of the most spectacular sights in Lebanon is in the Bekaa Valley. About half an hour from the main Beirut to Damascus highway is **Baalbek**. Situated at the top of the valley, this series of temples to Jupiter, Bacchus and Venus are some of the most awe-inspiring monuments anywhere. Columns over 20 metres high and over 2 metres in girth, stone blocks over 1000 tonnes in weight and elaborate engravings must be seen. These pagan temples are on a site probably dating back to Phoenician times but really developed by the Romans. In fact the Romans maintained and developed the site for several hundred years and in the latter stages of the Empire even tried to delete traces of paganism and show Christian images.

Between the 7th century AD and present times the city and its temples suffered from invading Arabs, Mongols and earthquakes. In the last two hundred years German, French and Lebanese scholars and archaeologists have tried to preserve this amazing site.

While in Baalbek visit the Palmyra Hotel where a record of the visitors is kept. The visits of presidents, crowned heads of Europe, military chiefs and musicians are all documented. Better still, be around for the International music festival when the most famous maestros, soloists, bands and orchestras descend on this unlikely spot.

While in the Bekaa valley why not stop at Zahlé and visit the riverside restaurants and try out the Lebanese food at its best, with some of the local specialities.

Visit the old **Ksara Caves** and see where for centuries one of Lebanon's finest wines has been stored – and why not do some tasting! (see chapter 9, p111). Also worth a visit is Chéle au Kefraye in Kefraye village for their wine.

Anjaar

Also in the valley and of great historical significance is the Umayyad town of **Anjaar**. Built in the 8th century AD this inland trading town was only discovered about 60 years ago. It has been well preserved and is the earliest known Islamic location in Lebanon. There will be few if any visitors and it is a unique experience to wander around these old columns and streets.

Beit Eddine (half day outing)

Beit Eddine: The palace built by Emir Bashir Shehab between 1790 and 1830 – a beautiful example of Lebanese Ohoma? period up in the hills in the village of Beit Eddine. On the way there, visit Deir El-Kamir, the administrative capital of Mount Lebanon during that period.

The Cedars

Famous for thousands of years, the **Cedars of Lebanon** are now all but extinct. A few of these huge trees, which have become the symbol of Lebanon (on the flag), can be seen in the north of the country near Bcharré. These trees, which had grown in forests throughout the country and which were such an important building material for thousands of years, used in Egypt for example, are now reduced to a handful of preserved 'monuments' to be viewed as a tourist attraction.

This area has now become the centre for skiing and is also the location for wealthy Lebanese to build

10

magnificent summer villas. Summer resorts like **Ehden** and **Bcharré** are now sophisticated spots with hotels and all amenities. The area is also famous for its various mountain monasteries. (see chapter 6, p79)

Shopping in Lebanon

Any traveller whether tourist or executive will always want to take a little souvenir back home as a memento. Lebanon is not really somewhere you can expect to take home tacky 'Made in China' knick knacks. Indeed more readily available but less affordable would be an Armani suit or a Gucci bag, etc. Such designer goods are everywhere and eagerly bought by wealthy Lebanese.

Designer Goods

One of the most affordable souvenirs has to be the **wine** or *arak*. Visit supermarkets and select your favourite tipple from racks of wine neatly laid out in their various vintages: the better the year, the higher the price – not surprisingly! I must caution the visitor, however, that as good as *arak* tastes in Lebanon it never quite tastes the same at home. There is something about the ambiance of the country that seems to make any food and wine seem like 'ambrosia' and 'nectar'!

Wine and Arak

10

Some gold or silver perhaps. This, too, is much sort after and purchased by the Lebanese. There are many shops selling all kinds of **jewellery**, which is made locally by skilled craftsmen – usually Armenians.

Jewellery

Visitors to Baalbek may pick up some unique **glass** and **brassware**. Visitors to Byblos can buy some samples of **fossilised fish** of varying sizes. **Leather** goods and **brass** and **copper** are also available. **Rugs** from Iran can be bought by the knowledgeable and wealthy visitor.

10

Lebanese Jewellery

My first visit to Beirut just after the war was full of surprises. At that time there was still a lot of rubbish and rubble littering some areas. I could never get over the sight of extremely elegantly dressed and bejewelled men and women emerging from amongst this squalor.

I was further amazed when I had the opportunity to meet a craftsman who made these decorations for the wealthy of the country. I was led from street level to the second basement in an ordinary block of flats in the city. Passing through two massive steel doors we entered a small workshop with half a dozen men working at benches. I was able to inspect the work and was also shown some of the pieces, which had been finished recently. The owner opened a large wall safe and took out several boxes – diamonds, tiaras, necklaces and sets of jewellery were displayed. I picked up one box, one of the more modest ones and asked how much. 40,000 US dollars I was told. I was then told that there was no shortage of buyers for such baubles, especially during the war, when these trinkets had been bought by loving partners as consolation gifts for enduring the difficulties of the conflict.

Appendix One

International Dialling Code for Lebanon – 00 961

Area Codes

Central Beirut	01
Syria	02
Cell phone	03
Jal el Dib	04
Baabda	05
Tripoli	06
Sidon and Tyre	07
Bekaa Valley	08
Jounieh	09

Emergency numbers

		Beirut
Civil Defense	125	
Fire Department	175	310105
Telephone Information	20	
International Dialing Services	100	
Police	160	425250
Red Cross	145	323345
Ambulance		865561
Tourist Police		343209

	Tripoli	Sidon
Police	430950	
Red Cross	602510	
Ambulance	602510	722532

Beirut Airport

Information:	**t:** 01. 628 000
Management	**t:** 01. 628 195/7
Customs	**t:** 01. 629 160/ 629 420
General Security	**t:** 01. 629 150/2

Credit Card Emergencies

American Express
Gefinor
t: (01) 747 111   **f:** (01) 749 577

Diners Club
Sin El-Fil
t: (01) 491 576   **f:** (01) 483 186

Master Card
Al-Mawarid Bank
Hamra
t: (01) 350 585   **f:** (01) 314 340

A1

Banque Libano-Francaise
Hamra
t: (01) 392 240   **f:** (01) 399 689

Credit Card Services Co
Hamra
t: (01) 742 555   **f:**01. 352 281

Fransabank
Hamra
t: (01) 747 597   **f:** (01) 341 275

Visa
Arab Bank Plc.
Riad Solh
t: (01) 981 152   **f:** (01) 980 803

Internet Service Providers

There are many of these and their numbers increase
regularly. Some of those available are:

Cyberia
t: (01) 744 101   **w:** www.cyberia.net.lb

Libancom
t: (01) 877 202   **w:** www.libancom.com.lb

Terranet
t: (01) 577 511   **w:** www.terr.net.lb

Hotels in Lebanon

Greater Beirut:

Alexandre
Ashrafieh
t: (01) 200 240   **f:** (01) 201 118

Albergo Relais & Chateaux
Achrafieh
t: (01) 339 797   **f:** (01) 339 999

Bayview Hotel
Ain Mreisseh
t: (01) 373 090   **f:** (01) 373 091

Beau Rivage
Ramlet El-Baida
t: (01) 01. 785 741   **f:** (01) 809 000

Beirut Marriott Hotel
Jnah
t: (01) 840 540   **f:** (01) 840 345

A1

Mercure Berkeley
Hamra
t: (01). 346 032　　　　*f:* (01) 341 777

Le Bristol
Mme Curie Street
t: (01) 351 400　　　　*f:* (01) 351 400

Cadmos
Ain Mreisseh
t: (01) 374 892　　　　*f:* (01) 374 898

Casa d'Or
Hamra
t: (01) 347 850　　　　*f:* (01) 347 840

Cavalier
Hamra
t: (01) 352 635　　　　*f:* (01) 347 681

Crown Plaza
Hamra
t: (01) 754 755　　　　*f:* (01) 749 555

Gefinor Rotana Hotel
Gefinor
t: (01) 371 888

Holiday Inn-Dunes
Verdun
t: (01) 792 111　　　　*f:* (01) 792 333

Holiday Inn-Martinez
Ain Mreisseh
t: (01) 368 111　　　　*f:* (01) 370 333

Imperial Suites Hotel
Raoucheh
t: (01) 862 781　　　　*f:* (01) 790 689

La Cigale
Zalka
t: (01) 893 441　　　　*f:* (01) 898 773

Le Meridien Commodore
Hamra
t: (01) 350 400　　　　*f:* (01) 350 400

Le Vendôme Intercontinental
Ain Mreisseh
t: (01) 369 280　　　　*f:* (01) 369 280

A1

Legend
Verdun
t: (01) 801 062   *f:* (01) 807 238

Marble Tower
t: (01) 346 260

Mövenpick
t: (01) 869 666   *f:* (01) 809 326

Marriott
t: (01) 840 540

Mayflower
t: (01) 340 580

Phoenicia
Minet El-Hosn
t: (01) 369 100   *f:* (01) 369 101

Riviera
Corniche El-Manara
t: (01) 373 210   *f:* (01) 365 239

Sheraton Coral Beach
Jnah
t: (01) 859 000   *f:* (01) 859 006

Sofitel Le Gabriel
Ashrafieh
t: (01) 203 700   *f:* (01) 320 094

Summerland
Jnah
t: (01) 858 000   *f:* (01) 856 666

Mount Lebanon / North:

Royal Park Hotel
Ain Saadeh
t: (04) 873 100   *f:* (04) 872 700

Colibri
Baabdat
t: (04) 820 402   *f:* (04) 820 153

Al-Bustan
Beit Meri
t: (04) 870 400   *f:* (04) 972 980

Beit Meri Hotel
Beit Meri
t: (04) 972 360   *f:* (04) 972 512

A1

A1

Grand Hotel Naas
Bikfaya
t: (04) 982 629   *f:* (04) 980 113

High Hill
Bikfaya
t: (04) 984 200   *f:* (04) 982 686

Bologna Grand Hotel
Bois de Bologne
t: (04) 295 100   *f:* (04) 295 143

Bellevue Palace
Broummana
t: (04) 865 000   *f:* (04) 963 022

Garden
Broummana
t: (04) 960 579   *f:* (04) 960 259

Le Crillon
Broummana
t: (04) 960 221   *f:* (04) 960 163

Primotel
Broummana
t: (04) 963 700   *f:* (04) 963 022

Printania Palace
Broummana
t: (04) 960 416   *f:* (04) 960 415

Russli
Broummana
t: (04) 960 015   *f:* (04) 960 016

Mount Lebanon/South:

Shouf Touristic Center
Baakline
t: (05) 301 273

Barouk Palace
Barouk
t: (05) 240 251   *f:* (05) 240 253

Mir Amine Palace
Beiteddine
t: (05) 503 065   *f:* (05) 501 315

Four Points Sheraton
Bhamdoun
t: (05) 260 300   *f:* (05) 260 310

North Lebanon:

Chbat
Bcharré
t: (06) 672 672   *f:* (06) 671 237

Alpine Hotel
Cedars
t: (06) 671 057

L'Auberge des Cèdres
Cedars
t: (06) 671 526   *f:* (06) 671 526

Mon Refuge
Cedars
t: (06) 678 050

Hotel Saint Bernard
Cedars
t: (06) 678 100   *f:* (06) 678 101

Belmont
Ehden
t: (06) 560 102   *f:* (06) 560 159

Ehden Country Club
Ehden
t: (06) 560 651   *f:* (06) 560 645

Grand Hotel Abchi
Ehden
t: (06) 560 001   *f:* (06) 561 103

La Mairie
Ehden
t: (06) 560 108   *f:* (06) 560 108

1st Class Al Naoura
Tripoli
t: (06) 401 651   *f:* (06) 401 625

Quality Inn
t: (06) 211 255

Villa Nadia
t: (06) 432 513

South Lebanon:

Mounes
Khaizarane
t: (07) 666 657   *f:* (07) 671 016

A1

Government Rest House
Tyre
t: (07) 740 677   *f:* (07) 345 163

Bekaa Valley:

Palmyra
Baalbek
t: (08) 370 011   *f:* (08) 370 305

Chtaura Park Hotel
Chtaura
t: (08) 540 011   *f:* (08) 542 686

Khreizat Al-Hotel
Khreizat
t: (08) 645 188   *f:* (08) 596 056

Masharef Saghbine
Saghbine
t: (08) 671 200   *f:* (08) 670 362

Al Rihab
Zahlé
t: (08) 806 017

Grand Hotel Kadri
Zahlé
t: (08) 813 920   *f:* (08) 813 920

Kesrouan:

Regency Palace Hotel
Adma
t: (09) 854 000   *f:* (09) 854 854

Hotel Bzoummar
Bzoummar
t: (09) 902 731   *f:* (09) 902 953

L'Auberge de Faqra
Faqra
t: (09) 300 501   *f:* (09) 300 610

Chateau d'Eau
Faraya
t: (09) 321 424

Saint Giorgio
Faraya
t: (09) 720 720   *f:* (09) 720 720

A1

Ahiram
Jbail
t: (09) 540 440   *f:* (09) 944 726

Byblos Sur Mer
Jbail
t: (09) 942 983   *f:* (09) 944 859

Aquarium
Jounieh
t: (09) 936 858   *f:* (09) 936 859

Arcada Marina
Jounieh
t: (09) 915 546   *f:* (09) 935 956

Beverly Beach
Jounieh
t: (09) 900 255   *f:* (09) 916 637

Dallas
Jounieh
t: (09) 937 720   *f:* (09) 914 301

Nirvana
Laqlouq
t: (01) 200 019   *f:* (01) 336 007

Shangrilla
Laqlouq
t: (01). 200 019   *f:* (01) 336 007

Montemar
Maameltein
t: (09) 851 624   *f:* (09) 851 628

Vanda
Maameltein
t: (09) 830 108   *f:* (09) 936 206

Auberge Suisse
Ouyoune El-Simane
t: (09) 953 841   *f:* (09) 953 841

Saint Antonio
Dallas
t: (09) 937 720

Jammal
Dallas
t: (01) 217 793

A1

Mzaar Inter-Continental
Dallas
t: (09) 340 100   ***f:*** (09) 340 101

Saint Rock
Reifoun
t: (09) 950 076   ***f:*** (09) 950 077

Century Park Hotel
Zouk Mikael
t: (09) 219 000   ***f:*** (09) 219 000

Portemilio Suite Hotel
Zouk Mikael
t: (09) 933 300   ***f:*** (09) 933 300

Zoukotel
Zouk Mikael
t: (09) 215 900   ***f:*** (09) 215 906

Hospitals

Abou Jaoudeh Hospital
Jal El-Dib
t: (04) 716 000

Al Arz Hospital
Zalka
t: (01) 876 770

Al Iman Hospital
Aley
t: (05) 555 970

American University Hospital
Hamra
t: (01) 350 000

Barbir Hospital
Barbir
t: (01) 652 915

Beirut General Hospital
Ramlet El-Baida
t: (01) 850 213

Bhaness Hospital
Bhaness
t: (04) 983 770

Dallaa Hospital
Saida
t: (07) 725 181

A1

Hammoud Hospital
Saida
t: (07) 723 888

Haykal Hospital
Koura
t: (06) 430 600

Hopital du Sacré-Coeur
Hazmieh
t: (05) 457 112

Hopital Libanais Geitaoui
Achrafieh
t: (01) 449 401

Hopital Notre Dame des Secours
Jbeil
t: (09). 944 255

Hopital Notre Dame du Liban
Jounieh
t: (09) 937 401

Hopital Pasteur
Jounieh
t: (09) 912 747

Hopital Fouad Khoury
Hamra
t: (01) 344 882

Hotel Dieu de France
Achrafieh
t: (01) 422 970

Karam Hospital
Achrafieh
t: (01) 200 400

Khalidy Hospital
Ras Beirut
t: (01) 340 247

Labib Medical Center
Saida
t: (07) 720 333

Makassed Hospital
Tarik El-Jdideh
t: (01) 646 590

A1

Mazloum Hospital
Tripoli
t: (06) 430 325

Middle East Hospital
Ramlet El-Baida
t: (01) 809 555

Monla Hospital
Tripoli
t: (06) 600 111

Najjar Hospital
Hamra
t: (01) 340 626

Nini Hospital
Tripoli
t: (06) 432 811

Rizk Hospital
Achrafieh
t: (01) 200 800

Sahel General Hospital
Haret Hreik
t: (01) 858 333

St. Georges Hospital
Achrafieh
t: (01) 321 700

Ste. Thérèse Hospital
Hadeth
t: (05) 463 100

Trad Hospital
Clemenceau
t: (01) 369 494

Airlines

Aeroflot
Gefinor Center
t: (01) 739 596

Air Algérie
Gefinor Center
t: (01) 741 391

Air Canada
Verdun
t: (01) 811 680

A1

Air China
Sin El-Fil
t: (01) 500 248

Air France
Achrafieh
t: (01) 740 300

Hamra
t: (01) 740 300

Air India
Sanayeh
t: (01) 736 620

Alitalia
Hamra
t: (01) 340 280

Austrian Airlines
Ain Mreisseh
t: (01) 343 620

British Airways
Gefinor Center
t: (01) 747 777

Cathay Pacific Airways
Gefinor Center
t: (01) 741 391

CSA (Transas) Airlines
Ain Mreisseh
t: (01) 368 950

Cyprus Airways
Achrafieh
t: (01) 200 886

Egyptair
Gefinor Center
t: (01) 741 402

Emirates Airlines
Gefinor Center
t: (01) 739 042

Gulf Air
Achrafieh
t: (01) 323 332

A1

Iberia Airlines
Sanayeh
t: (01) 749 831

JAT (Pan Asiatic)
Gefinor Center
t: (01) 747 748

KLM
Hamra
t: (01) 746 599

Kuwait Airways
Gefinor Center
t: (01) 739 485

Lufthansa
Gefinor Center
t: (01) 347 006

Malaysia Airlines
Gefinor Center
t: (01) 741 344

Malev – Hungarian Airlines
Kantari
t: (01) 363 159

Middle East Airlines
Airport
t: (01) 737 000

Verdun
t: (01) 865 442

Gefinor Center
t: (01) 737 000

Olympic Airways
Hamra
t: (01) 340 285

Philippines Airlines
Hamra
t: (01) 342 415

Qatar Airways
Ramlet El-Baida
t: (01) 810 375

A1

Royal Jordanian Airlines
Hamra
t: (01) 379 990

Jal El-Dib
t: (04) 710 207

Sin El-Fil
t: (01) 493 320

Sabena
Riad El-Solh
t: (01) 985 255

Saudi Arabian Airlines
Hamra
t: (01) 349 100

Singapore Airlines
Hamra
t: (01) 351 237

Sudan Airways
Hamra
t: (01) 739 074

Swiss International
Ain Mreisseh
t: (01) 985 254

Tarom Romanian Airlines
Hamra
t: (01) 742 966

Turkish Airlines
Gefinor Center
t: (01) 741 391

Jal El-Dib
t: (04) 717 137

Yemenia
Gefinor Center
t: (01) 741 395

Yugoslav Airlines
Gefinor Center
t: (01) 741 391

A1

Automobile/Limousine Rentals:

Arabia
Badaro
t: (01) 615 882

Auto Tour
Jdeideh
t: (01) 888 222

AVIS Lebanon
Ashrafieh
t: (01) 611 000

Kantari
t: (01) 366 662

Raoucheh
t: (01) 861 614

Budget Rent-A-Car
hamra
t: (01) 740 741

Capital Rent-A-Car
Hazmieh
t: (05) 455 460

City Car
Ras Beirut
t: (01) 803 931

Dallah Rent-A-Car
Bir Hassan
t: (01) 840 774

Dana Rent-A-Car
Verdun
t: (03) 282 298

Europcar
Sin al Fil
t: (03) 282 298

Hala Rent-A-Car
Airport
t: (01) 692 444

Kaslik
t: (09) 219 000

Le Vendôme
t: (01) 369 280

A1

Sami El-Solh
t: (01) 393 904

Hertz Lebanon
Sami El-Solh
t: (01) 427 283

Jet
Ras Beirut
t: (01) 340 380

Lena Car
Ain Mreisseh
t: (01) 480 480

Sin El-Fil
t: (01) 480 480

Lion Rent-A-Car
Jounieh
t: (09) 831 308

More Rent-A-Car
Hamra
t: (01) 746 500

Option Car Rental
Corniche El-Mazraa
t: (01) 301 226

Pico Rent-A-Car
Sami El-Solh
t: (03) 820 728

Prince Car
Jdeideh
t: (01) 882 748

Sin El-Fil
t: (01) 510 317

Prestige
Raoucheh
t: (01)863 222

Jounieh
t: (09) 910 953

Speedy
Manara
t: (01) 741 574

A1

Sunny Rent-A-Car
Hamra
t: (01) 740 011

Thrifty Marriott Hotel
Jnah
t: (01) 840 540

Royal Plaza Hotel
Raoucheh
t: (03) 380 201

Sin El-Fil
t: (01) 510 100

V.I.P. Limousine
Ashrafieh
t: (01) 294 600

Taxis
Allo Taxi
t: (01) 366 661

Beirut Taxi
t: (01) 805 418

City Taxi
t: (01) 397 903

Lebanon Taxi
t: (01) 353 152

Embassies
Algeria
Jnah
t: (01) 826 711

Argentina
Starco Area
t: (01) 987 900

Armenia
Rabieh
t: (04) 418 860

Australia
Ras Beirut
t: (01) 374 701

Austria
Ashrafieh
t: (01) 217 448

A1

Bahrain
Manara
t: (01) 367 975

Belgium
Baabda
t: (05) 920 551

Bolivia
Dora
t: (01) 240 711

Brazil
Baabda
t: (05) 921 255

Bulgaria
Raoucheh
t: (01) 961 352

Canada
Jal El-Dib Highway
t: (04) 521 163

Syria
t: (0211) 6116851

Chile
Naccache
t: (04) 418 670

China
Ramlet El-Baida
t: (01) 850 314

Colombia
Jal El-Dib
t: (04) 712 646

Korea South
Baabda
t: (05) 922 151

Cuba
Ain El-Tineh
t: (01) 805 025

Czech Republic
Baabda
t: (05) 468 763

A1

A1

Denmark
Ain Mreisseh
t: (01) 364 264

Egypt
Ramlet El-Baida
t: (01) 862 932

Finland
Hamra
t: (01) 802 275

France
Museum District
t: (01) 616 730

Germany
Rabieh
t: (04) 914 444

Greece
Naccache
t: (04) 521 700

Hungary
Fanar
t: (01) 898 840

India
Kantari
t: (01) 372 811

Indonesia
Baabda
t: (05) 924 682

Ireland
Verdun
t: **(01) 863 040**

Iran
Bir Hassan
t: (01) 821 230

Italy
Hamra
t: (01) 340 225

Japan
Baabda
t: (05) 922 001

Jordan
Baabda
t: (05) 922 500

Kuwait
Bir Hassan
t: (01) 822 515

Libya
Verdun
t: (01) 806 314

Malta
Ashrafieh
t: (01) 201 973

Mexico
New Naccache
t: (04) 418 870

Morocco
Ain El-Tineh
t: (01) 862 966

Netherlands
Ashrafie
t: (01) 204 663

Norway
Hamra
t: (01) 365 704

Pakistan
Raoucheh
t: (01) 863 041

Philippines
Raoucheh
t: (01) 791 092

Poland
Hamra
t: (01) 345 278

Qatar
Raoucheh
t: (01) 865 271

Romania
Baabda
t: (05) 924 848

A1

A1

Russia
Mar Elias
t: (01) 300 041

Saudi Arabia
Koraitem
t: (01) 860 351

Spain
Hadath
t: (05) 464 120

Sudan
Mme Curie Street
t: (01) 353 270

Sweden
Ashrafieh
t: (01) 339 505

Switzerland
Ashrafieh
t: (01) 324 129

Tunisia
Hazmieh
t: (05) 457 430

Turkey
Rabieh
t: (04) 520 929

United Arab Emirates
Jnah
t: (01) 857 000

United Kingdom
Beirut Central District
t: (01) 990 400

United States of America
Aoucar
t: (04) 417 774

Uruguay
Jounieh
t: (09) 636 529

Venezuela
Zalka
t: (01) 888 701

Yemen
Bir Hassan
t: (01) 852 688

Yugoslavia
Sanayeh
t: (01) 739 633

Courier Services

All Transport Agency
Badaro
t: (01) 395 000

Aramex International Courier
Gefinor
t: (01) 484 166

Sin El-Fil
t: (01) 484 166

Ain al-Mreisseh
t: (01) 361 797

Beyrouth Courses
Dekouaneh
t: (01) 499 636

DHL
Avenue Sami El-Solh
t: (01) 382 700

Hamra
t: (01) 746 460

DHL Worldwide Express
Sami El-Solh
t: (01) 390 900

Falcon Aviation Services
Hamra
t: (01) 340 289

Federal Express
Riad El-Solh Square
t: (01) 987 000

International Courier Services
Hamra
t: (01) 803 530

Libanpost
t: (01) 629 629

A1

Midex Liban
Badaro
t: (01) 385 090

On Time
Jardin Jesuites
t: (01) 442 777

Rapidco
Sin El-Fil
t: (01) 480 186

Road Net
Sin El-Fil
t: (01) 489 480

Sky Net
Sin El-Fil
t: (01) 489 480

TNT
Hamra
t: (01) 342 176

Top Speed
Khandak El-Ghamik
t: (01) 653 259

United Couriers
Ashrafie
t: (01) 201 575

UPS-United Parcel Services
Ashrafie
t: (01) 218 575

24 Hour Pharmacies

Kaddoura Pharmacy
Gefinor Center
t: (01) 739 593

Berty Pharmacy
Ashrafie
t: (01) 330 033

Mehio Pharmacy
Talat Khayat
t: (01) 816 126

Mazen Pharmacy
Corniche Al-Mazraa
t: (01) 313 362

Pharmacie Chehab
Bachoura
t: (01) 663 600

Soubra Pharmacy
Ain El-Tineh
t: (01) 866 266

Summerland Pharmacy
Jnah
t: (01) 304 830

Pharmacie Embassy
Ashrafie
t: (01) 204 248

Banks
ABN Amro Bank
Dora
t: (01) 241 145

Hamra
t: (01) 736 004

Ashrafie
t: (01)329 210

American Express Bank
Sin El-Fil
t: (01) 480 040

Gefinor
t: (01) 341 879

Clemenceau
t: (01) 749 313

Ashrafie
t: (01) 337 833

Arab Bank
Riad El-Solh
t: (01) 980 040

Hamra
t: (01) 340 630

Verdun
t: (01) 800 013

Sin El-Fil
t: (01) 510 355

A1

Audi Investment Bank
Dora
t: (01) 888 720

Banca Di Roma
Tabaris
t: (01) 204 681

Hamra
t: (01) 347 779

Dora
t: (01) 894 071

Bank of Beirut
Clemenceau
t: (01) 739 940

Mar Elias
t: (01) 305 571

Achrafieh
t: (01) 204 606

Bank of Beirut & the Arab Countries
Clemenceau
t: (01) 360 460

Hamra
t: (01) 341 280

Verdun
t: (01) 790 394

Achrafieh
t: (01) 201 780

Bank of Kuwait & the Arab World
Ain Tineh
t: (01)865 295

Hamra
t: (01) 346 348

Zalka
t: (01) 884 450

Achrafie
t: (01) 215 635

Haret Hreik
t: (01) 559 927

A1

Bank of Tokyo
Riad El-Solh
t: (01) 997 766

Banque Audi
Ashrafie
t: (01) 253 515

Hamra
t: (01) 341 491

Verdun
t: (01) 805 805

Gefinor
t: (01) 743 400

Riad El-Solh
t: (01) 980 211

Sin El-Fil
t: (01) 490 301

Banque de l'Industrie et du Travail
Saifi
t: (01) 580 051

Riad El-Solh
t: (01) 980 170

Ashrafieh
t: (01) 200 521

Gefinor
t: (01) 739 051

Mar Elias
t: (01) 369 630

Banque du Liban (Central Bank)
t: (01) 750 000

Banque du Liban et d'Outre-Mer
Hamra
t: (01) 340 015

Verdun
t: (01) 343 425

Sanayeh
t: (01) 346 042

Place Sassine
t: (01) 200 147

A1

A1

Fransabank
Hamra
t: (01) 340 180

Sodeco
t: (01) 200 845

Byblos Bank
Achrafieh
t: (01) 335 200

Hamra
t: (01) 341 539

Banque de la Mediterranée
Verdun
t: (01) 866 925

Mar Elias
t: (01) 314 655

Credit Libanais
Av.Charles Malek
t: (01) 200 028

Hamra
t: (01) 342 954

Citibank
Gefinor
t: (01) 738 400

HSBC
Ashrafie
t: (01) 377 477

Hamra
t: (01) 742 832

Standard Chartered Bank
Sanayeh
t: (03) 397 739

SGLEB
Sin El-Fil
t: (01)480 927

Hamra
t: (01) 350 020

Accountants

priceWaterhouse Coopers
t: (01) 203 420

KPMG

Chamber of Commerce and Industry
Spears Street
Sanayeh
Beirut.
t: (01) 353 390-1-2/ 744 160-1

Tripoli
t: (06) 432 790

Sidon
t: (07) 720 123

Zahle
t: (08) 817 681

Ministries

Culture	*t:* 371 497
Economy and Trade	*t:* 340 540
Environment	*t:* 524 999
Finance	*t:* 424 720
Foreign Affairs	*t:* 200 469
Health	*t:* 615 701
Industry	*t:* 427 047
Labour	*t:* 556 832
Oil	*t:* 427 985
Tourism	*t:* 354 764

A1

Appendix Two

Appendix two

Arabic – The Language of Lebanon

Most expatriates will learn some Arabic while they are living in the Middle East. Some will become proficient, others will merely learn to "get by". The English language is widely used or at least understood in Lebanon, as is French (most Lebanese are proficient in Arabic, English and French). Indeed it is embarrassing to sit in a restaurant in Beirut and to discuss the menu in English with the waiter, to find that he will pass to the next table and carry on a similar conversation in French or Italian with manifest ease.

It is suggested that in order to speak Arabic, it is easier to learn the written text at the same time – it is then possible to read road or shop signs, newspapers, etc. Practising to speak their language is very difficult, since your Lebanese conversant will simply revert to your mother tongue in the interest of being understood. A good practice ground is in taxis (good captive audiences if you persevere) where you can try out your Arabic while the driver responds in English.

A few words of Arabic are definately worth having, however. For one thing it enables the business executive to give the impression of fluency and this discourages Arabic discussions taking place during a meeting. It is also a small courtesy to be able to say 'Good Morning', 'How are you?', etc. and comforting to be able to give directions to drivers: 'Turn left', 'After half an hour', etc.

Arabic is a phonetic language, but there are two extra 'sounds' used in the language that are very difficult for a Western tongue to handle. One is the harsh glottal stop (as in Cockney 'wa-er' for 'water', indicated in the following pages with a hyphen) and the other sound similar to someone clearing their throat (like the *ch* in the Scottish 'loch', shown here as *kh*). To master these sounds requires some practice and some patience from the listener; without these sounds some words become indistinguishable from others leading to considerable confusion and possibly embarrassment. One other possible source of consusion is the lack of the letter P in their language – replaced with a B when rendering foreign proper names in Arabic.

A2

Transliteration of Arabic is always a subject of debate. The following does not adhere to any hard and fast rules, and simply seeks to approximate to whoat might hear, or how a an English language reader might attempt to reproduce the sounds.

Good-morning	*sabaah al khayr*
Reply	*sabaah al noor*
	(have a bright one)
or	*sabaah al ward*
	(let it smell like roses)
Good-afternoon	*masaa al khayr*
Reply	*masaa al noor*
Hello	*marhaba*
Goodbye	*ma-a salaama*
Goodnight	*missaa al khayr*
(when leaving at night or going to bed)	
Reply	*wa inta min ahl al khayr*
How are you?	*keefak (to a man), keefik (to a woman)*
Fine, thank you	*quais, al humdulillah*
	(Good, thanks be to God)
What's your name?	*shoo ismak? (m) shoo ismik? (f)*
My name is....	*ismi ....*

Thank you	*shukran*
I do not understand	*mish (not) faahim*
Do you speak English?	*tahki ingleezi?*
What ....?	*shu...?*
What is this?	*shu haida?*
Where ....?	*wayn...?*
Where is the bathroom?	*wayn al hammam?*
How much (money)?	*kaddesh?*
How many?	*kam?*
Why?	*laysh?*
Here	*hoon*
There	*hinnaak*
God willing	*insha-allah*
(frequently used in many circumstances)	
Yes	*na-am*
No	*la*
And	*wa*

Never mind	*ma-a leesh*
I mean...	*ya-ani...*

(trendy expression, tends to irritate if used too often)

Again	*kamaan*
OK	*maashi*
No problem	*maa fi mushkila*

(all-purpose phrase, e.g. when you have reversed into someone's car)

It is possible	*mumkin*
It is not possible	*mish mumkin*
Finish, stop	*khalaas*

(as in 'You have reversed into my car!')

Excellent	*tammaam* or *mazboot*
Only, stop, enough	*bass*

(as in 'Stop reversing into my car!')

Congratulations	*mabrook*
Me	*anna*
Foreigner	*ajnabi*
Broken	*maksoor* (m) *maksoora* (f)
Up	*fowq*
Down	*taht*
After	*ba'ad*
With	*ma-a*
With sugar	*ma-a sooccar*
Without	*bedoon*
Without milk	*bedoon haleeb*
Tea	*shai*
Coffee	*kahwa*
Electricity	*kahraba*
No electricity	*maa fee kahraba*

Locations

Airport	*mataar*
Bridge	*jisir*
Embassy	*safaara*
British Embassy	*safaara Britaniyya*
Ambassador	*safeer*
Home, house	*bayt*
My (your) home	*bayti (baytak)*
My home is your home	*bayti baytak*
Hospital	*mustashfa*
Hotel	*funduq* or *hotel*
Phoenicia Hotel	*funduq Phoenicia*
Bazaar, shops	*suq*
Office	*maktab*

A2

My office	*maktabi*
School	*madrassa*
Square	*medan* or *saha*
Al-Borj Square	*sahat Al-Borj*
Street	*shaari-a*
Lebanon	*Lubnan*

Directions

Ahead, straight on	*alla tool*
Right	*yameen*
Left	*shimal*
After	*ba-ad*
Near	*jamb*
Stop here	*wa-if hoon* (here good)

Money

Lebanese pound	*leera*
Change	*frata*
No change	*maa fee frata*
How much?	*ad aysh*
Too much	*kiteer*

Numbers

one	*wahad*
two	*itnayn*
three	*tellaata*
four	*arba-a*
five	*khamsa*
six	*setta*
seven	*saba-a*
eight	*temaanya*
nine	*tissa-a*
ten	*-ashra*
eleven	*ihdash*
twelve	*itnash*
thirteen	*tellatash*
fourteen	*arbaa-tash*
fifteen	*khamastash*
sixteen	*settash*
seventeen	*sabaa-tash*
eighteen	*temantash*
nineteen	*tissaa-tash*
twenty	*ishereen*
thirty	*tellateen*
forty	*arbaareen*
fifty	*khamseen*

A2

sixty	*setteen*
seventy	*sabaa-een*
eighty	*temaneen*
ninety	*tissa-een*
one hundred	*miyye*
one thousand	*alf*
two thousand	*alfayn*

Time

Today	*al yom*
Later	*ba-adayn*
Now	*halla*
('I'll do it immediately' becomes *haalan*)	
Tomorrow	*bukra*
After tomorrow	*ba-ad bukra*
Yesterday	*imbarrah*
Before yesterday	*awal imbaarrah*
Morning	*subh*
Afternoon	*ba-ad i dohr*
Night	*billayl*
Sunday	*il ahad* (*wahad* - one)
Monday	*il itenayn* (*itnayn* - two)
Tuesday	*ittellaata* (*tellata* - three)
Wednesday	*il arbaa* (*arbaa* - four)
Thursday	*il khamees* (*khamsa* - five)
Friday	*il jumma-a*
Saturday	*issabt*
One o'clock	*issaah wahad*
Two o'clock	*issaah itnayn*
Half past three	*issaah tellata wa nuss*

A2

appendix three
commercial support
for US companies

Appendix three

Directory of Export Assistance Centers

Cities in capital letters are centres which combine the export promotion and trade finance service of the Department of Commerce, the Export-Import Bank, the Small Business Administration and the Agency of International Development.

Two of the largest and most useful export associations in the US are ExportZone U.S.A. and The Export Institute of the U.S.

ExportZone U.S.A.
218 W. San Marcos Blvd
Suite # 106-176
San Marcos, CA 92069
U.S.A.
❑ Tel: 760 295 1652; fax: 760 295 1656
E-mail: [info@exportzone.com]

&

The Export Institute of the United States of America
6901 W.84th St., Suite 359
Minneapolis, MN 55438
Tel: 800 943 3171; fax: 952 943 1535
Email: [jrj@exportinstitute.com]

A3

ALABAMA

Birmingham, Alabama - George Norton, Director
950 22nd Street North, Room 707, ZIP 35203
t: : (205) 731-1331   *f:* (205) 731-0076

ALASKA

Anchorage, Alaska - Charles Becker, Director
550 West 7th Ave., Suite 1770, ZIP: 99501
t: (907) 271-6237   *f:* (907) 271-6242

ARIZONA

Phoenix, Arizona - Frank Woods, Director
2901 N. Central Ave., Suite 970, ZIP 85012
t: (602) 640-2513   *f:* (602) 640-2518

CALIFORNIA - LONG BEACH
Joseph F Sachs, Director
Mary Delmege, CS Director
One World Trade Center, Ste. 1670, ZIP: 90831
t: (562) 980-4550   **f:** (562) 980-4561

CALIFORNIA - SAN JOSE
101 Park Center Plaza, Ste. 1001, ZIP: 95113
t: (408) 271-7300   **f:** (408) 271-7307

COLORADO - DENVER
Nancy Charles-Parker, Director
1625 Broadway, Suite 680, ZIP: 80202
t: (303) 844-6623   **f:** (303) 844-5651

CONNECTICUT
Middletown, Connecticut - Carl Jacobsen, Director
213 Court Street, Suite 903 ZIP: 06457-3346
t: (860) 638-6950   **f:** (860) 638-6970

DELAWARE
Served by the Philadelphia, Pennsylvania U.S. Export
Assistance Center

FLORIDA - MIAMI
John McCartney, Director
P.O. Box 590570, ZIP: 33159
5600 Northwest 36th St., Ste. 617, ZIP: 33166
t: (305) 526-7425   **f:** (305) 526-7434

GEORGIA - ATLANTA
Samuel Troy, Director
285 Peachtree Center Avenue, NE, Suite 200
ZIP: 30303-1229
t: (404) 657-1900   **f:** (404) 657-1970

A3

HAWAII
Honolulu, Hawaii - Greg Wong, Manager
1001 Bishop St.; Pacific Tower; Suite 1140
ZIP: 96813
t: (808) 522-8040   *f:* (808) 522-8045

IDAHO
Boise, Idaho - James Hellwig, Manager
700 West State Street, 2nd Floor, ZIP: 83720
t: (208) 334-3857   *f:* (208) 334-2783

ILLINOIS - CHICAGO
Mary Joyce, Director
55 West Monroe Street, Suite 2440, ZIP: 60603
t: (312) 353-8045   *f:* (312) 353-8120

INDIANA
Indianapolis, Indiana - Dan Swart, Manager
11405 N. Pennsylvania Street, Suite 106
Carmel, IN, ZIP: 46032
t: (317) 582-2300   *f:* (317) 582-2301

IOWA
Des Moines, Iowa - Allen Patch, Director
601 Locust Street, Suite 100, ZIP: 50309-3739
t: (515) 288-8614   *f:* (515) 288-1437

KANSAS
Wichita, Kansas - George D. Lavid, Manager
209 East William, Suite 300, ZIP: 67202-4001
t: (316) 269-6160   *f:* (316) 269-6111

KENTUCKY
Louisville, Kentucky - John Autin, Director
601 W. Broadway, Room 634B , ZIP: 40202
t: (502) 582-5066   *f:* (502) 582-6573

A3

LOUISIANA - DELTA
Patricia Holt, Acting Director
365 Canal Street, Suite 1170
New Orleans ZIP: 70130
t: (504) 589-6546   *f:* (504) 589-2337

MAINE
Portland, Maine - Jeffrey Porter, Manager
c/o Maine International Trade Center
511 Congress Street, ZIP: 04101
t: (207) 541-7400   *f:* (207) 541-7420

MARYLAND - BALTIMORE
Michael Keaveny, Director
World Trade Center, Suite 2432
401 East Pratt Street, ZIP: 21202
t: (410) 962-4539   *f:* (410) 962-4529

MASSACHUSETTS - BOSTON
Frank J. O'Connor, Director
164 Northern Avenue
World Trade Center, Suite 307, ZIP: 02210
t: (617) 424-5990   *f:* (617) 424-5992

MICHIGAN - DETROIT
Neil Hesse, Director
211 W. Fort Street, Suite 2220, ZIP: 48226
t: (313) 226-3650   *f:* (313) 226-3657

MINNESOTA - MINNEAPOLIS
Ronald E. Kramer, Director
45 South 7th St., Suite 2240, ZIP: 55402
t: (612) 348-1638   *f:* (612) 348-1650

MISSISSIPPI
Mississippi - Harrison Ford, Manager
704 East Main St., Raymond, MS, ZIP: 39154
t: (601) 857-0128   *f:* (601) 857-0026

A3

MISSOURI - ST LOUIS
Randall J. LaBounty, Director
8182 Maryland Avenue, Suite 303, ZIP: 63105
t: (314) 425-3302   **f:** (314) 425-3381

MONTANA
Missoula, Montana - Mark Peters, Manager
c/o Montana World Trade Center
Gallagher Business Bldg., Suite 257, ZIP: 59812
t: (406) 243-2098   **f:** (406) 243-5259

NEBRASKA
Omaha, Nebraska - Meredith Bond, Manager
11135 "O" Street, ZIP: 68137
t: (402) 221-3664   **f:** (402) 221-3668

NEVADA
Reno, Nevada - Jere Dabbs, Manager
1755 East Plumb Lane, Suite 152, ZIP: 89502
t: (702) 784-5203   **f:** (702) 784-5343

A3

NEW HAMPSHIRE
Portsmouth, New Hampshire - Susan Berry, Manager
17 New Hampshire Avenue, ZIP: 03801-2838
t: (603) 334-6074   **f:** (603) 334-6110

NEW JERSEY
Trenton, New Jersey - Rod Stuart, Director
3131 Princeton Pike, Bldg. #4, Suite 105, ZIP: 08648
t: (609) 989-2100   **f:** (609) 989-2395

NEW MEXICO
New Mexico - Sandra Necessary, Manager
c/o New Mexico Dept. of Economic Development
P.O. Box 20003, Santa Fe, ZIP: 87504-5003
FEDEX:1100 St. Francis Drive, ZIP: 87503
t: (505) 827-0350   **f:** (505) 827-0263

NEW YORK
t: (212) 466-5222   **f:** (212) 264-1356

NORTH CAROLINA - CAROLINAS
Roger Fortner, Director
521 East Morehead Street, Suite 435, Charlotte, ZIP: 28202
t: (704) 333-4886   *f:* (704) 332-2681

NORTH DAKOTA
Served by the Minneapolis, Minnesota Export Assistance Center

OHIO - CLEVELAND
Michael Miller, Director
600 Superior Avenue, East, Suite 700
ZIP: 44114
t: (216) 522-4750   *f:* (216) 522-2235

OKLAHOMA
Oklahoma City, Oklahoma - Ronald L. Wilson, Director
301 Northwest 63rd Street, Suite 330, ZIP: 73116
t: (405) 608-5302   *f:* (405) 608-4211

OREGON - PORTLAND
Scott Goddin, Director
One World Trade Center, Suite 242
121 SW Salmon Street, ZIP: 97204
t: (503) 326-3001   *f:* (503) 326-6351

PENNSYLVANIA - PHILADELPHIA
Rod Stuart, Acting Director
615 Chestnut Street, Ste. 1501, ZIP: 19106
t: (215) 597-6101   *f:* (215) 597-6123

PUERTO RICO
San Juan, Puerto Rico (Hato Rey) - Vacant, Manager
525 F.D. Roosevelt Avenue, Suite 905
ZIP: 00918
t: (787) 766-5555   *f:* (787) 766-5692

A3

RHODE ISLAND
Providence, Rhode Island - Vacant, Manager
One West Exchange Street, ZIP: 02903
t: (401) 528-5104, *f:* (401) 528-5067

SOUTH CAROLINA
Columbia, South Carolina - Ann Watts, Director
1835 Assembly Street, Suite 172, ZIP: 29201
t: (803) 765-5345   *f:* (803) 253-3614

SOUTH DAKOTA
Siouxland, South Dakota - Cinnamon King, Manager
Augustana College, 2001 S. Summit Avenue
Room SS-44, Sioux Falls, ZIP: 57197
t: (605) 330-4264   *f:* (605) 330-4266

TENNESSEE
Memphis, Tennessee - Ree Russell, Manager
Buckman Hall, 650 East Parkway South, Suite 348
ZIP: 38104.
t: (901) 323-1543   *f:* (901) 320-9128

A3

TEXAS - DALLAS
LoRee Silloway, Director
P.O. Box 420069, ZIP: 75342-0069
2050 N. Stemmons Fwy., Suite 170, ZIP: 75207
t: (214) 767-0542   *f:* (214) 767-8240

UTAH
Salt Lake City, Utah - Stanley Rees, Director
324 S. State Street, Suite 221, ZIP: 84111
t: (801) 524-5116   *f:* (801) 524-5886

VERMONT
Montpelier, Vermont - Susan Murray, Manager
National Life Building, Drawer 20, ZIP: 05620-0501
t: (802) 828-4508   *f:* (802) 828-3258

VIRGINIA
Richmond, Virginia - Helen D. Lee Hwang, Manager
400 North 8th Street, Suite 540, ZIP: 23240-0026
P.O. Box 10026
t: (804) 771-2246   *f:* (804) 771-2390

WASHINGTON - SEATTLE
David Spann, Director
2001 6th Ave, Suite 650, ZIP: 98121
t: (206) 553-5615   *f:* (206) 553-7253

WEST VIRGINIA
Charleston, West Virginia - Harvey Timberlake, Director
405 Capitol Street, Suite 807, ZIP: 25301
t: (304) 347-5123   *f:* (304) 347-5408

WISCONSIN
Milwaukee, Wisconsin - Paul D. Churchill, Director
517 E. Wisconsin Avenue, Room 596, ZIP: 53202
t: (414) 297-3473   *f:* (414) 297-3470

WYOMING
Served by the Denver, Colorado U.S. Export Assistance
Center

A3